OTHER BOOKS BY JAY R. LEACH

How Should We Then Live

Behold the Man

The Blood Runs Through It

Drawn Away

Give Me Jesus

A
LIGHT
UNTO
MY
PATH

Embracing the Truth
of God's Word

JAY R. LEACH

 www.trafford.com

North America & international
toll-free: 1 888 232 4444 (USA & Canada)
fax: 812 355 4082

In honor of my father, the Reverend Curtis A. Leach
who set the standard high
and lived a life worthy of the prize
of the high call of God in Christ Jesus.
His shoes are too big to fill,
but hid footprints will most definitely be followed.

CONTENTS

SECTION 1—YOUR WORD IS TRUTH

Chapter 1   God's Word, His [Gps] 3
Chapter 2   Truth or Consequences 9
Chapter 3   The Christian's Treasure 16
Chapter 4   The Abiding Word 28

SECTION 2—WHAT GOD REQUIRES

Chapter 5   The Spirit Filled Church 45
Chapter 6   Remember Who You Are 57
Chapter 7   The Church's Highest Priority 66

SECTION 3—TRUTH IN CHRISIS

Chapter 8   The Promise of the Father 73
Chapter 9   Receving the Promise of the Father........................80
Chapter 10   When Power comes to Church 92

SECTION 4—GIVE YOURSELF AWAY

Chapter 11   Take It to the Streets 105
Chapter 12   Have a Contagious Spirit.......................................111
Chapter 13   Seeing Tomorrow Today...116
Chapter 14   Contend for the Faith...126

SECTION 5—TO GOD BE THE GLORY

Chapter 15   Strengthening the Right Hand of God 145
Chapter 16   Everyone Must Witness 151

INTRODUCTION

"But when the Helper comes, who I shall send to you from the Father, the Spirit of truth who proceeds from theFather, He will testify of Me. ". . . . He will guide you into all truth . . ."

(John 15:26; 16:12)

On the Andy Griffith show one day, Opie and another boy were arguing, the little boy took three steps backward drew a line on the ground and dared Opie to cross it. Opie looked around at his friends who were nudging him on. He stepped across the line and the bully took off. Christian Philosopher Francis Schaeffer warned this nation in the 1970's that the line had been drawn—and unless we changed as a nation, someday we would wake up and find out that the America we once knew is gone. After four decades we have all awakened to find, that day is here.

We have crossed the line, and the bully is not retreating. In fact it seems that in crossing the line we were actually duped into moving [through spiritual ignorance] down a river of no return. The institutional church in America is also being swept right along with the nation by a powerful secular media and mainstream culture that is pushing the local churches and forcing a collapse of the church culture; as they struggle with a myriad of critical issues that must be addressed in order to understand contemporary change in reality: because of rejection of Christianity for humanism, relationships, relativism, multiculturalism, the new tolerance, responsibility, racial and gender-based inequities, sexuality, spirituality and many others. This brief assessment and related shifts provide a picture of the enormous challenge facing the church today.

Many congregations and church leaders have after assessing the situation, retreated into their four walls and created church programs as substitutes for the Christ-given mission to "make disciples" and "thy kingdom come." These churches huddle together treating anyone or anything not like them as the enemy. In abandoning their mission they have actually abandoned their real identity and reason for existence. Others have gone to another extreme; while claiming to continue the mission to "make disciples," they chose to sell out to the secular culture. Their worship service is a period of entertainment with the objectives to "be happy" "feel good" and "have a good time."

In 1998, when Magdalene and I founded the Bread of Life Bible Institute a Barna poll reported that 20 million born again Christians turned off by the institutional church had left the church. A recent poll increased that figure to 115 to 117 million. The prediction is that that figure will double in the next decade. Many of these Christians have found refuge in the Bread of Life and like ministries across America. As a result of this group not only are we establishing other campuses (7 in several States), but also the planting of churches (5) and networking with other restoration ministries and churches. Some of the people in the institutional church have names for us, radical, rebel, troublemaker, etc. The point is because the institutional church has given up their reason for existing; God did not change His plan. He simply made an "end-run" on the institutional church [where the members serve the church]—and the people (115 million) hit the streets to continue His mission "to make disciples and extend His kingdom on earth." There is hope! If you want to be a part of the present move of God:

- First, realize that the situation is beyond human strength [*the* flesh] to solve.
- Second, the church must realize that "Nothing is too hard for God!" He has already sent the Spirit of truth to guide the church. Acknowledge Him church!
- Third, regroup, retrain, and get rid of the access baggage of tradition and return to Christ's grace of the Holy Spirit's

supernatural anointing, power, gifts, signs and wonders established [to continue] in the early church.

- Fourth, return to God's GPS, the Spirit-guided *truths* of the Bible to keep you on the right path.
- Fifth, repent, and return to your Christ-given mission and reason for existing, to "make disciples" and "extend the kingdom of God."

We must preach and teach the true gospel of Christ which is the *power of God* unto salvation (1 Corinthians 15:2-3). The church must dispel the "fear of the Holy Spirit" through anointed teaching and training in the Doctrine of the Holy Spirit: His Person, His work in the church and the world, and His work in you. Renew your minds through the truths of God's Word and pray that every Christian come to the realization that we are a supernatural people "a kingdom of kings and priests" capable of great exploits *in* Christ Jesus (see Romans 12:1-6). Clearly, to *influence* the nation through the Spirit and God's Word demands that we be vigilant in monitoring the forces of change through the eyes and power of the Holy Spirit. Only then can we receive and put in place truthful responses based on God's Word that are helpful and not harmful; only then are we positioned to have influence for God's glory.

A look at history reveals how other nations of the past have traveled this same path. Each once stood as *the* World Power just as America stands today. The Scripture informs us of their ends, and predicts what will be America's destiny if there is no national repentance, renewal, and return to serving the Living God:

"The wicked
Shall
Be turned into
Hell,
And all the nations
That forgets God"
(Psalm 9:17).

This passage and similar ones confirm the promise of the New Testament affirmation that a day of final judgment is coming in which the righteousness of God will be displayed and the sin and wickedness of unrepentant humankind will finally receive their just punishment" (see Matthew 25:31-46; Revelation 14:10, 11).

Yet, God has provided a way for the righteous to escape the coming judgment. He has given us, the Holy Spirit and the Holy Bible, a lamp unto our feet and a light unto our path. The Holy Spirit is the Lamp and the truth of God's Word is the Light of revelation and understanding to empower us to be able to illuminate the world's darkness. I'm excited! My goal in writing is to help you to get on board!! A study guide is provided at the end of each chapter to aid you in walking out those truths revealed to you in this resource.

Jay R. Leach

SECTION 1

YOUR WORD IS TRUTH

Chapter 1

GOD'S WORD, HIS [GPS] KEEPS US ON THE RIGHT PATH

*"In the beginning was the Word, and the Word was with God, and **the Word was God . . .**" "**And the Word became flesh and dwelt among us**"*

(John 1:1, 14).

Jesus is Lord! He is the Word, He is the Christ, He is the Savior, and He is the Head of the Body, the Church. In these last days there are those who deny all of the above; and are fervently working with Satan to smite any and all knowledge of the same, Jesus Christ, from the public square.

The Apostle Paul wrote, *"The **wrath of God** is **revealed** from heaven against all ungodliness and unrighteousness of men, who **suppress the truth** in unrighteousness, because what may be known of God is **manifest in them,** for God has shown it to them. For since the creation of the world His invisible attributes are **clearly seen,** being **understood** by the things that are made, even His eternal power and Godhead, so that they are **without** excuse, because, although **they knew God,** they did not **glorify Him, as God,** nor were **thankful,** but became futile in their thoughts, and their foolish hearts are darkened. **Professing to be wise,** they became fools, and changed the **glory of the incorruptible God into an image** made like corruptible man—and birds and four-footed animals and creeping thing. Therefore **God also gave them up** to uncleanness, in the lusts of their hearts, to dishonor their bodies among themselves,* *who exchanged the **truth of God for a lie,** and worshipped and served the creature rather than the Creator, who is blessed forever. Amen"* (Romans 1:18-25). [Emphasis is mine throughout].

The wrath of God here is not some impulsive outburst of anger aimed at people whom God is upset with or hate; but following closely behind many tragedies and major catastrophic events, this idea seems to always surface with saints and sinners alike. He is still God and He is still Sovereign! The MacAuthur Study Bible notes on Romans 1 offers two ways God reveals His wrath:

- Indirectly through the natural consequences of violating His universal moral law.
- Directly through His personal intervention.

Further it explains the most graphic revelation of God's holy wrath and hatred against sin when He poured out divine judgment *on* His Son on the cross.

God has various kinds of wrath:

- Eternal wrath, which is hell.
- Eschatological wrath, which is the final Day of the Lord.
- Cataclysmic wrath like the destruction of Sodom and Gomorrah.
- Consequential wrath, which is the principle of sowing and reaping.
- Abandonment wrath, which is removing restraint and letting people go to their sins (for examples of this wrath, see Psalm 81:11, 12; Proverbs 1:23-31; and also see Hosea 4:17 to pursue their sin and vv. 24-32), its consequences.[1]

God has revealed Himself to humanity through the evidence from:

- Conscience (see 1:19; 2:14).
- Creation (see 1:20).
- The truth of God's Word (The Holy Bible).

Therefore through these three elements, humankind is without excuse (see 1:20).

Research reveals that Christianity in America has become more diluted, marred and spiritless with each new generation. In Christian circles many opinions and suggestions are floated in answering the [why?] for this degradation. However, the truth of this matter is spelled out in God's Word. Scripture after Scripture proves that this lack of reverence, conformity in thought, word and deed are the results of people choosing to oppose, choosing to suppress, and choosing to resist the truths of God's Word even unto blood in some instances. Many at the same time holding fast to their sins. The Apostle John addressing this condition said,

"And this is the condemnation,
That the light has come into the world,
And men loved darkness
Rather than light
And
Does not come to the light,
Lest his deeds be exposed"
(John 3:19-20).

Sometime ago, while removing several old boards from the ground around my storage shed; I noticed upon picking up each board, I exposed the activities in the little world of bugs and other little critters underneath. In just a few seconds all of them had disappeared as they scurried to find some other dark place to hide as if their very existence depended upon it. They hate the light. Though light has come into the world more and more people, including many holding membership in the local churches are getting familiar with and comfortable in the darkness of sin. People in this corrupted culture in America are becoming like fish in the ocean—to them water is all there is! Many of our citizens at all levels are coming to believe that pleasure, evil, and corruption are the norm and to be expected as part of life; to them that's all there is. The recent exposure of the IRS scandal, the Supreme Court's striking down proposition 8 in California wherein through public voting seven million citizens voted that marriage was between one man and one woman, substituting the media and public opinion **over** the expressed desires of the people in this matter? The Trevon Martin case is a prime example of God's moral law being overruled by the legal law of man. All of that should be a wake up call to the church. The possibility of this type of overreach to forbid our right to preach the *true* gospel of Christ or to use certain words and phrases in a like manner are closer than you think. Then, there is the unethical behavior permeating the leadership in many of the nation's major institutions and services. Prime examples of this error are present at all echelons of leadership.

Through rejection of biblical Christianity and spiritual ignorance, more and more immoral activities and corruption have become acceptable to the main stream of America and regretfully to many in the local institutional churches—resulting in more children and young adults growing up in secular environments and never exposed fo truth or the true Gospel of Jesus Christ; therefore they have no idea who Jesus is or the truth of God's Word about Him. In his sermons, at some point Evangelist Billy Graham would insert, the Bible says, "Christ died for the whole world!" Isn't that suppose to be the "cry" of the whole church?

The Scripture affirms, "God so loved the world that He gave His only begotten Son, that whoever believes in Him should not perish but have everlasting life" (John 3:16). The Son of God's total mission is bound up in this supreme love of God for this evil, sinful "world" of humanity that is in rebellion against Him (see John 6:32, 51; 12:47).

His love includes YOU! Repent, turn around and give your heart to Him today. He promises eternal life to those who receive Him. Come to Jesus! If you are already saved let this message be a reminder that we are our brother's keeper. Win someone to Christ. A day of reckoning is on the horizon. The Apostle John reports, "Then I saw a great white throne and Him who sat on it, from whose face the earth and the heaven fled away. And I saw the dead, small and great, standing before God, and the books were opened. And another book was opened, which is the Book of Life.

And the dead were judged according to their works, by the things which were written in the books. Death and Hades delivered up the dead who were in them. And they were judged, each one according to his [or her] works. Then Death and Hades were cast into the lake of fire. This is the *second death.* And anyone not found written in the Book of Life was cast into the lake of fire" (Revelation 20:11-15). Those individuals who are saved are born twice, [physical and Spiritual] and only die once. Those who are born once [physical] will die twice (see Revelation 20:14; Romans 10:9-10; John 3:16).

These verses describe the final judgment of all the unbelievers of all ages (see Matthew 10:15; 11:22, 24; 12:36, 41, 4; John 12:48; Acts 17:31; 24:25; Romans 2:5, 16; Hebrews 9:27; 2 Peter 2:9; 3:7; Jude 6). In His great grace and mercy God insures that we know the full story, through the truth of the Scripture for our existence here on earth; and what is expected of us here. Then the Bible also tells us what happens to us when we depart this life. Actually, we see that our existence continues in eternity.

Think about it, a million years after our death or rapture, we will still exist. Where we spend eternity is to our own choosing. Heaven or the lake of fire the choice is yours. Jesus came and died that we might enjoy an abundant life here and a glorious eternity with Him (see John 10:10).

There are those who claim that you can have this abundant life and heaven without the new birth, but Jesus said, "You must be born again, otherwise you cannot see the kingdom of heaven." He further explains, "Except a man [or woman] is born of the water and of the Spirit, he or she cannot enter the kingdom of God" (see John 3:3, 5). Today's challenges must be countered by Spirit-filled Christians welding the power of Pentecost, [the Holy Spirit and the truth of God's Word]. Let there be no doubt, Pentecost set the pattern for the church continuously throughout the Church Age. The brackets are mine throughout. Thy Word is a lamp unto my feet.

STUDY GUIDE: CHAPTER 1

GOD'S WORD, [GPS] KEEPS US ON THE RIGHT PATH

1. Jesus is Lord and He is the _____.

2. God revealed Himself through the evidence from _____, _____, and _____.

3. Romans 1 offer two ways God reveals His wrath.

   1.
   2.

4. Anyone not found written in the Book of Life was _____ into the _____ of _____.

5. Jesus came and died that we might enjoy the _____ _____ here and a glorious future with Him.

Chapter 2

TRUTH OR CONSEQUENCES

".... For without Me you can do nothing"
(1 John 15:5).

During a recent dental appointment, as I sat in the chair, I overheard a couple discussing the problems of big government in Washington. As I sat there I began to think that bigness is one of the major problems in the church today. However, that bigness shows up in a number of unscriptural customs, traditions and secular ideas hindering the spirituality of the institutional church today. In fact many of these things became hindrances to spiritual growth when they were no longer useful means to ends. Instead of discarding them, the church adopted them to became ends in themselves. As we will see in a later chapter, these *created* means actually canceled out the mission of the church to "make disciples." Additionally, the church displaced the kingdom here on earth. This condition appears when humanity becomes confused, spiritually cold, and unscriptural in their vision casting without Christ. This certainly holds true for our present governmental leadership in the church. We see deterioration in all of our national institutions from the home and family to all foundational institutions. This happens more rapidly as rejection of biblical Christianity becomes more the norm. No matter what the world philosophers and soothsayers have to offer, Christ is the truth of God's Word and therefore He is the standard for all conduct and behavior. Attempting to deny the existence of Christ, who actually created it all and holds it all together is ludicrous; especially for those who claim to be His.

When the Example Fades Away

The New Testament Church began at Pentecost with "fire" from heaven. The pattern for Pentecost was set in keeping with the "fire" from heaven on the altar of the Tabernacle and "fire" from heaven in Ezekiel's temple (see Ezekiel 43:13-27). I believe the "fire" depicts *God with us* in the Tabernacle, and the Temple, but from Pentecost to the rapture, the fire depicts *God in us* (see 1 Corinthians 3:16); who make up the body of Christ, the Church. Like the Old Testament priests, today as priests we are responsible for keeping the fire [of the Holy Spirit] burning (see 1 Peter 2:5, 9).

Jesus Christ had much to say to His disciples concerning the founding and establishing of His church. Christ is the Rock upon which the Church is founded because:

- Through Him [**only**] comes faith in God for salvation from sin.
- Through Him comes love to the human heart, which makes humans view personality as sacred.
- God is the Creator of humanity's physical and spiritual being.
- He is the [**only**] hope concerning the future.
- To insure that the work He was leaving to His apostles and disciples (120 men and women) to do; He told them to wait in Jerusalem for the arrival of the Holy Spirit, the Spirit of Truth.
- He would fill them empowering them to speak boldly the *truth of God's Word* as His witnesses to the world (see Acts 1:8; 2:1-4) and guide them into all truth (see John 14:16-18, 25-26; 16:13).

The filling with the Spirit is a repeated reality of Spirit-controlled behavior that God commands *all believers* to maintain (see Ephesians 5:18). Notice, the waiting disciples:

- All became Spirit-centered, Spirit-empowered, and Spirit-guided.

- All became filled with the Holy Spirit (Acts 2:4).
- All were now partakers of the divine nature.
- All were no longer imitators of Christ.
- Christ's actual life passed into their lives (Romans 5:10).

The authentic Church of the Living God is a supernatural community under King Jesus, who is the Head. An identity was established between the disciples and the Spirit [which includes His present day disciples] to the extent that their hands were His hands, reaching out to fallen humanity; their feet were His feet, running errands of mercy; their eyes were His eyes, to reveal divine love and compassion.

The wonderful and fearfully-made earthen vessel was fully realized. The Holy Spirit resides in the regenerated spirit as the new holy of holies in which the divine life was to reside. It's important to note at this point the temple made of stone is replaced by the newly established temple of flesh and blood. In this relationship the human body was and is referred to as the *"temple of the Holy Spirit"* (see 1 Corinthians 6:19). In God's redemptive plan, the body is lifted to a new level of dignity. It is not a social club, society or fantasy in which lusts and passions run rampart in uncontrollable conduct. Instead, the body is the cathedral in which the Holy Spirit resides.

On the Day of Pentecost "tongues of fire" unloosed the tongues of the disciples and turned them into flaming swords. Here was human voice speaking God's truth; human speech touched by the Spirit's inspiration, a human organ used as a channel of superhuman power. **Now He was talking through them!** As true born again biblical Christians nothing less is expected of us today—equipped we are ready to tackle the challenges!

This is the assessment from the Word of God concerning those who are His. With the foundational doctrine of the incarnation, the crucifixion, the resurrection of Christ and the pouring out of the Holy Spirit at Pentecost, the young church was born and **equipped with the indwelling Spirit and the Word of God** to go into all the world with the entrusted Gospel [the Good news of Christ].

A Lamp unto My Feet

The Apostle Paul explains that the Good News of Christ *"is the power of God to salvation for everyone who believes"* (Romans 1:16). The Greek word for salvation used by Paul literally means *"deliverance"* or *"preservation"* lending the idea of a rescue from the power and dominion of sin.

Jesus had already given His apostles the Great Commandments to set [*the Christian's character and conduct*] for His church to "love your God with all your heart, with all your soul, and with all your mind this is the first Commandment. And the second is like it: "You shall love your neighbor as yourself" (Matthew 22:37-39). The Great Commission to set [*the Church's marching orders*] from Christ Himself:

> "Go into all the world
> To make disciples
> Baptizing them
> Teaching them
> To observe all things
> whatsoever
> **I have
> commanded** you"
> (Matthew 28:18-19).

Study also: Mark 16:15-18; Luke 24:47-49; John 20:21). The Church's mandate today is the same mandate that Christ gave the early church to:

- Love the Lord with all your heart.
- Love your neighbor as yourself.
- Win you neighbor to Christ **[through the authentic truth of God's Word]** (see Romans 10:9-10; John 3:16).
- Make disciples equip them for [mature] life and service **[through the authentic truth of God's Word]**.

Truth of God's Word is Key

The Psalmist referred to the Word of God as a lamp *[the Holy Spirit]* unto his feet and light is the authentic *[truth of God's Word]* (see Psalm 119:105). We must remember that the Bible does not simply contain the Word of God, the Bible is the Word of God, penned by "holy men of God . . . as they were moved by the Holy Spirit" (see II Peter 1:21). In reference to the importance of God's Word; the Apostle Peter assures us, *"Grace and peace be multiplied to you in the knowledge of God and of Jesus our Lord, as His divine power has given to us all things that pertain to life and godliness, through the **knowledge of Him [means a personal sharing of life with Him based on repentance from sin and a personal faith in Him]** who called us by glory and virtue, by which have been given to us exceedingly great and precious **promises,** that through these you may be **partakers of the divine nature, [having been born again and now in Christ]** having escaped the corruption [old sinful nature]* that is in the world through lust"* (2 Peter 2-4; also see 2 Corinthians 5:17). The added emphasis and brackets are mine throughout.

Those who love Christ will prove their devotion to Him in His service—by **seeking** and **obeying God's Word.** Here's the payoff. Jesus said, *"If you keep My commandments, you will abide in My love, just as I have kept My Father's commandments and abide in His love"* (John 15:10). When the church, [true disciples] abide in Christ's love—John assures us in verses 7-11 that:

- Our prayers will be effective.
- We glorify God in our fruit bearing.
- We demonstrate our discipleship.
- We experience Christ's peace and joy within.

Paul admonishes Timothy, *"And the things that you have heard from me among many witnesses, commit these to **faithful** men who will be able to teach others also"* (2 Timothy 2:2). Timothy was to take the truths of God's Word he had learned from Paul and teach it to other faithful men—men and women with *proven* spiritual character and giftedness, who would in turn pass those truths on to another generation. That's God's way of supplying His church, multiplication. From Paul to Timothy to faithful men [and women] to others encompass four generations of godly leaders. The process of spiritual reproduction initiated and successfully modeled by the early church, is to continue until the Lord returns.

STUDY GUIDE FOR CHAPTER 2

TRUTH OR CONSEQUENCES

1. Jesus told His disciples to wait in Jerusalem for the _____
   _____.

2. In the Old Testament God was _____ us and in the New
   Testament God is _____ us.

3. Salvation is the _____ to salvation for
   everyone who believes.

4. _____ is God's way of supplying His church.

5. To what kind of men was Timothy to commit _____
   _____?

Chapter 3

THE CHRISTIAN'S TREASURE

"They were all filled with the Holy Spirit"
(Acts 2:4).

God highly respected the Church when He bestowed upon the body of Christ the right and privilege to possess His truth and go into the entire world giving forth His Words of Life. The success of the church does not depend on a sophisticated or educated ministry, a large budget, or influential members. Neither should the Church follow a traditionally set program. Instead the church must be *responsive* and *open* to the guidance of the Holy Spirit fitted for the demands of the moment:

"Not by might, nor by power,
but by My Spirit
says the Lord of hosts"
(Zechariah 4:6).

If the Church would recapture the irresistible drive of the early apostolic Church, their fruitfulness and effectiveness will be repeated.

Pentecost—the Pattern for the Church

"They were all filled with the Holy Spirit" (Acts 2:4). This proclamation embraces the Source of the hidden power of

biblical Christianity and its secret weapon. Jesus said of this secret weapon: "Whom the world cannot receive, because it neither sees Him nor knows Him" (John 14:17).

The Church is empowered with this secret weapon, the Holy Spirit. The Apostle Peter preached on the Day of Pentecost and the Scripture says, "When they heard this, they were cut to the heart, and said to Peter and the rest of the apostles, "Men and brethren, what shall we do?" Then Peter said to them, "**Repent**, and let every one of you be baptized in the name of Jesus Christ for the remission of sins; and you shall receive the **gift** of the Holy Spirit. For the **promise** is to you and to your children, and to all who are afar off, as many as the Lord our God will call" (Acts 2:37-39).

Someone has summed up the two-way relationship between the Holy Spirit and the believer this way: the believer <u>cannot</u> do it without the Holy Spirit; and the Holy Spirit <u>will not</u> do it without the believer!

By My Spirit

Since it is an established truth that the church is empowered by the Holy Spirit; then any Christian or local church that does not depend on the Holy Spirit's empowerment, knowledge, and obedience of God's Word for success is doomed to **death.** The Christian community must yield continually to the Spirit's control; likewise each Christian must also yield his or her personality and every area of daily life. An example of this failure can be found in the church at Sardis (Revelation 3:1-6). Sardis was one of the seven representative churches that Christ showed to the apostle John on the Isle of Patmos. Each church depicted the churches condition during various period of history between the Day of Pentecost and the Rapture.

The city of Sardis was the capitol of the Roman province of Lydia. During the early church period, Sardis was a wealthy and prosperous city. The name *Sardis* is from a Hebrew word meaning *"to those who have escaped,"* or *"remnant."* The period of time illustrated by this church was the Reformation, a time when many churches were marked by *outward ritualism* and *inward deadness.*[2]

When John wrote the letter to Sardis, it was a wealthy city, but degenerate. The attitude of the city was reflected in the death of its church. Like the city that smugly dwelt upon its past glory. Sardis *appeared* to be alive, but was dead. Like the city they thrived on past glory:

- The church of Sardis at one time had a good reputation and the members thought they had arrived. Like this church, many local churches and Christians go through life looking out of the rear-view mirror depending upon past successes (vv. 1-4).
- The members of the church thought there works impressed God.
- They were content in their beautiful church building located on the corner at Main Street and First Avenue.

Christ said of this church, *"I know your works, that you have a name that you are alive, but you are dead"* (Revelation 3:1). What was the cause of death?

- The church died because it relied on its past successes. The body which was once healthy had been neglected.
- The church died because it allowed sin to creep into the membership.
- The church died because it was not sensitive to its own *spiritual* condition. A period historian reported that over the course of many years the church had acquired a reputation for lax morals.
- The church died because it was confident that God was there because the building was magnificent and the members were well-dressed.

- The church died because like the people Paul described in his letter to Timothy: *". . . . Having a form of godliness but denying its power"* (2 Timothy 3:5). "Form" refers to *outward shape* or *appearance.*

Like the Pharisees, false prophets and teachers along with their followers are concerned with mere external appearances (see Matthew 23:25; Titus 1:16). Their outward form of Christianity and virtue makes them all the more dangerous.

A Wake up Call

Christ is telling the church to wake up and remain awake. The Church should be honest in its assessment and admit something is wrong.

- One of the major problems causing churches to die is allowing doctrinal error to slip into the membership. Who is doing the teaching?
- What do we believe? Correct doctrine is important.
- Do we have small groups? This strategy is good for bringing the membership to maturity.

Christ sternly warned, *"But if you do not wake up, I will come like a thief, and you will not know at what time I will come to you"* (Revelation 3:3). This message is going unheeded among many churches in this Nation today; facing the sudden judgment which God will bring upon them if they don't repent.

However, in the Church at Sardis, and in our own churches like Sardis—there are a *"few members who have not soiled their garments."* But many have (v. 4)! The majority of these people were in the Church but not really in the Lord. Christ's message is clear (see v. 3):

- Remember
- Hold fast
- Repent

They were to change their minds and move forward in the Christian faith to avert judgment (see Jude 3).

For those who were overcoming, who had not soiled their garments, Christ made a promise (vv. 4-6):

- They would walk with Him in white.
- They would be rewarded for their faithfulness, being true to the Lord.
- Their names would not be blotted out of the Book of Life.
- They would be certain of their salvation.
- They would be confessed before the Father and the angels.

Are you in a Sardis-type church today? Notice the profile:

- Some were spiritually dead (v. 1).
- Some were ready to give up spiritually (v. 2).
- Their works were not fulfilled or completed before God (v. 2).
- Many members in the church were defiled (v. 4).

I noticed the church programs and activities page in the local newspaper today. People are very active—but unless these activities are **produced by the Spirit of God,** nothing is being accomplished! Why would anyone think of going to war without their weapon, **[the Holy Spirit]**? The Sardis-type church is very popular today and misleading many, many people. Motivated to fill the pews, finances, and no questions asked on entry into the church have produced some churches with in-house sinners and hypocrites **[without spirit]** in high places. Some Churches even cater to some specific sins because of cultural pressure.

My wife and I often discuss our childhood Sunday schools and how long before graduating from High School our biblical world view for life was set. Though we were not raised in the same church we were blessed with Spirit-filled High School graded Sunday school teachers.

As a Bible teacher, I am constantly bombarded by people torn with the question, "should I remain or should I leave?" The greatest concern seems to be apathy and a lack of Spiritual knowledge of the **truth** of God's Word. Christ reminds the true believer of the importance of the **Holy Spirit, to be submissive to His control.** Emphasis is mine.

God's Truth versus Humanistic Philosophy

There is a growing tension between absolute truth and subjective truth. Humanistic philosophers deny absolutes. Spouting such thoughts as because there are no absolutes; there is no absolute truth, so truth is up to the individual to determine. Textbooks and training materials around the country reflect this humanistic view of truth.

Jesus said, ". . . . I am the Truth . . . ." Meaning there is absolute truth because God said so. Further that means His Word; the Holy Bible is also absolute truth. One of the tasks of the Holy Spirit who is the Spirit of Truth is to lead and teach believers all truth (see John 14:17). It is the Christians' duty to stand in and for the truth of God's Word. He said it and that ought to settle it as for as His children are concerned.

The Holy Spirit forms us through our new nature into Christ likeness. Again, it bears repeating we must depend totally on the Holy Spirit to reveal the truth and impart wisdom to use it. Only those who depend on the Holy Spirit please God.

Those who fail to appropriate and apply these truths will experience few, if any of the benefits and blessings that God intended for them. Additionally, they will no doubt become stumbling blocks both to themselves and the next generation.

Compromise

Any Christian accepting the humanistic philosophy of subjective truth over absolute truth will compromise biblical truth. Webster's New Explorer Dictionary defines compromise as a *settlement of differences by **mutual concessions*** [acts of yielding].[3] The Spiritual influence of God's Word over the past 50 or 60 years has deteriorated so drastically that the attitudes of most of our traditional institutions including some churches and families have actually yielded to political correctness and other concessions demanded by the mainstream and humanistic agenda.

Issues that were spoken of in whispers twenty or thirty years ago are headline news today. The phenomenal growth in the acceptance of same sex marriages and the promotion of cohabitation as a normal lifestyle has so eroded the cultural consciousness that compromise is the order of the day. Rejection of biblical truth and spiritual ignorance enables Satan to further his dark agenda in America and the Western world. In Scripture Satan is referred to as the prince of darkness [spiritual darkness].

Compromising or making concessions with humanistic standards; while at the same time rejecting the truth of God's Word is pathetic and the epitome of political correctness which is gross sin. Once a local church is contaminated with compromise, it loses its light. Jesus made this statement; Christians *"are the light of the world."* Therefore we should realize that the world is living in darkness—even though the people are continuously boasting of their enlightenment. There are many Scriptures to substantiate that fact: *"But you are a chosen people . . . . A people belonging to God . . . . Who called you out of darkness into the wonderful light"* (1 Peter 2:9).

Where is America now?

People the world over are beginning to speak of America in the past tense, as our top leadership at all levels moved by the cultural upheaval and mainstream media has helped lead this great country away from its godly heritage and biblical worldview. We are now experiencing an overwhelming downward spiral of evil manifested through:

- A spirit of lawlessness, permissiveness, rebellion, inclusiveness, and selfishness in this generation which is growing more diabolically violent. Why?

- We are experiencing open immoral actions in America that were openly "unthinkable" 30 or 40 years ago, but are very rapidly becoming the norm. Why?
- In the last 60 years biblically based values and virtues among young adult Americans have dropped from 65% to 4%. Why?
- Since 1973, 55 million recorded abortions have been performed in this country. Why?

In the history of humankind, there has **never** been a society whose moral values have deteriorated so rapidly, and in such a short period of time as those of the American people during the past 50 or 60 years. The other day as I watched the evening news every major network announced that the *"morning after pill"* is available over the counter with no age restrictions. One reporter commented, "They will soon be as common as aspirins." Not long ago, the breaking news was a portrait of Pope Francis constructed of condoms.

This total barrage of immoral agenda flies in the face of the body of Christ as the Christian community very slowly becomes familiar with the new tolerance, and its baby, acceptance of immoral acts clearly noted in God's Word to be abominations and open rebellion toward Him and humanity.

In this present age, people have begun to feel liberated to openly display and even promote their sins, not only by their lifestyles but also through every means available to everyone. The American mainstream media, many professors, politicians and even some church leaders promote this darkness of humanistic philosophies:

- Hedonism—states that, "pleasure is the chief good in life."
- Materialism—is preoccupation with material rather than intellectual and spiritual things.
- Multiculturalism—respects and understands all *cultures* and *lifestyles.* A multicultural person is open, to the pluralistic beliefs and lifestyles of all except those who cling to Judea-Christian values.

It seems that through these philosophies mainstream America is willing to give up every blessing that God bestowed upon this nation from its birth; especially our biblical worldview which leads to Christ and salvation. They are openly choosing death over life for instant gratification, sexual freedom and material goods. The Scripture said, *". . . . because, although they knew God, they did not glorify Him as God, nor were thankful, but became futile in their thoughts, and their foolish hearts were darkened"* (Romans 1:21).

People have been immersed in their culture all their lives, and like a fish in water it is hardest to see what is always before your eyes; and therefore, hardest to see what everyone accepts. Jesus explains in a parable how hard it is for people to break from their traditions, customs, and religions.

Jesus responding to this in Matthew 15:19 said, *"For out of the heart proceeds evil thoughts, murders, adulteries, fornications, thefts, false witnesses, and blasphemies."* As a person thinks in their heart, so is he or she. Thoughts get into the heart **naturally** through the five senses. Therefore, our actions and behavior are determined by what we take into hearts [mind, will and emotions] and let settle and take roots there. Satan attempts to keep everyone's mind pre-occupied with believing his deceptive lies:

- Have you to think that the winner of the battle at Calvary is undecided (see Genesis 3:15).
- Think that everything you are going through is because of some sin you've committed (see Romans 8:28).
- Think that God won't keep His promises (see Titus 1:2)
- Think that worldly thoughts are normal (see Romans 12:1-2).

He wants to keep you away from that that matters most [a renewed mind]. The Scripture admonishes, "Let this mind be in you, which was also in Christ Jesus" (Philippians 2:5).

Before any person can live right—he or she must think right about God, Christ, and the Holy Spirit, the blood of Jesus, the Word of God, and others (see Romans 12:1-2).

Marching to the Global Drumbeat

I read a story about a frog that landed in a pan of water and stayed until it boiled. Had the water been hot, the frog would have noticed and hopped out immediately. But the water felt cool at first, and the frog sensed no danger. The frog simply **relaxed** and **conformed** to the gradual change. Subdued by the rising water temperature it grew too sluggish to act. By the time the water actually boiled, the frog was dead.

Should we really be surprised at the success of today's [stealth] revolution in the culture? The new-paradigm message began to take root in academia soon; after prayer and Bible reading were outlawed in the schools in the early sixties, while the church was preoccupied with other pressing matters. The young people who led the counterculture became mainstream pacemakers in the seventies, eighties, and early nineties. Many of them became professors, teachers, leaders in government, and other areas of public service; including the church and mentors for today's professionals, while others wrote books and other publications that helped establish the new values.

As a student of history, I spend time researching the rise and fall of world powers. I find it fascinating that England, Spain and Portugal all stood at some point in history exactly where America stands today, the world's quickly fading last of the old (Big Four) super powers of recent times. All of them came on the scene for a while then slipped into obscurity—while trying to take care of all the people, naturally! God is speaking today through His written Word to all nations, *"The wicked shall be turned into hell and all nations that forget God"* (Psalm 9:17). A day of final judgment is coming in which the righteousness of God will be manifested and the wicked and unrepentant people and nations will finally receive their chosen punishment (see Matthew 25:31-46; Revelation 20:11-15).

Unless America **repents** and **returns** to the Living God and get rooted in the authentic **truth** of God's Word, Satan will continue to win spiritual battles in this country—**except we repent!** One of the most gracious promises God has made to His people is found in II chronicles 7:14: *"If my people which are called by my name, shall humble themselves, and pray, and seek my face, and turn from their wicked ways; **then will I hear** from heaven, and will forgive their sin, and heal their land."* While this Word was spoken to Israel, we receive the promises through our inheritance as the seed of Abraham (see Galatians 3:29). When we have knowledge of the truth; we know what promises to pray for.

STUDY NOTES: CHAPTER 3

THE CHRISTIANS SECRET WEAPON

1. The church must be _____ and _____
   to the guidance of the Holy Spirit.

2. The church of Sardis was marked by _____
   and _____.

3. The church of Sardis thought their _____
   impressed God.

4. The church of Sardis died because it was not sensitive to its own
   _____ condition.

5. What was Christ's message to overcomers?

6. There is a growing tension between _____ truth and
   _____ truth.

Chapter 4

THE ABIDING WORD

"I am the true vine, and My Father is the vinedresser. Every branch in Me that does not bear fruit He takes away; and every branch that bears fruit He prunes, that it may bear more fruit. You are already clean because of **the Word** *which I have spoken to you. Abide in m\Me, and I in you. As the branch cannot bear fruit of itself, unless it abides in the vine, neither can you, unless you abide in me.*

I am the vine, you are the branches. He who abides in Me, and I in him, bears much fruit; for without Me you can do nothing. If anyone does not abide in Me, he is cast out as a branch and withered; and they gather them and throw them into the fire, and they are burned. If you abide in Me, and **My Words** *abide in you, you will ask what you desire, and it shall be done for you. By this My Father is glorified, that you bear much fruit; so you will be My disciples.*

As the Father loved Me, I also have loved you; abide in My love. If you keep My Commandments, you will abide in My love, just as I have kept My Father's commandments and abide in His love.

These things I have spoken to you, that My joy may remain in you, and that your joy may be full. This is My commandment, that you love one another as I have loved you"

(John 15:1-12).

The Living Word

Jesus proclaimed seven statements found in the gospel of John claiming His deity. In John 15:1, He stated, *"I am the true vine,"* the final of these seven statements (see John 6:35; 8:12; 10:7, 9; 10:11, 14; 11:25; 14:6). In John 15:5 Jesus made it clear, **". . . . without Me you can do nothing."** Apart from Christ a believer cannot accomplish anything of permanent spiritual value.

In John 3:3 Jesus said, **"Unless one is born again, he cannot see the kingdom of God."** Spiritual formation produced by the Holy Spirit is necessary for salvation; whereby eternal life is imparted to the believer (study 2 Corinthians 5:17; Titus 3:5; 1 Peter 1:3, 1 John 2:29; 3:9; 4:7; 5:1, 4, 18). In the process of Spirit forming our *new nature* forms us into the likeness of Christ. This is accomplished through the Living Word as we obediently submit to the precepts of the written Word of God.

If we are not knowledgeable, diligently seeking righteousness, and hating what God hates, we will easily fall prey to Satan's deceiving spirits. "The Spirit clearly says, *"in the last days some will abandon the faith and follow deceiving spirits . . ."* (1 Timothy 4:1). The Bible bears out the fact that biblical Christianity comes from the heart. Notice:

- We *understand* from the heart (Acts 28:27).
- We *believe* from the heart (Romans 10:9-10).
- We *love* from the heart (Matthew 22:27).
- We *sing* from the heart (Colossians 3:13).
- We *obey* from the heart (Romans 6:17).
- We *speak* from the heart (Luke 6:45).
- We *pray* from the heart (Psalm 51:10-17).

The Abiding Word

Jesus said, "If you abide in Me and My words abide in you, you will ask what you desire, and it shall be done for you" (John 15:7). The term "abide" means to bear, endure, dwell, remain, and last.

The new birth which makes us one with Christ is a miracle of God's grace, and the purging of the branch is also a miracle of God's grace **through the Word;** but "abiding" is definitely the Christian's responsibility. The invitation of Jesus to the sinner is, "Abide in Me." Throughout the New Testament we are admonished to:

- "Be alert and watchful" (see 1 Peter 5:8).
- "Present your bodies a living sacrifice" (Romans 12:1).
- "Yield you members as instruments of righteousness" (Romans 6:13).
- "Abstain from all appearances of evil" (1 Thessalonians 5:22).
- "Have no fellowship with the unfruitful works of darkness" (Ephesians 5:11).
- "Whatever you do in word or deed, do all in the name of the Lord Jesus, giving thanks to God and the Father by Him" (Colossians 3:17).
- "Whether therefore you eat or drink, or whatever you do, do all to the glory of God" (1 Corinthians 10:31).

Abiding in Christ was established in our lives, so now His words abide in us as we diligently study and apply them to our lives. Paul summed it up when he told the elders of the church at Ephesus: "So now brethren, I commend you to God and to the Word of His grace, which is able to build you up" (Acts 20:32). It is God's Word, as we study, hear and apply it that it is able to abide within us building up and securing us in the most holy faith.

In his book *The Alternative to Christendom,* Craig A. Carter suggests that the church learn survival skills from the Jews. Though the majority of Jews rejected Jesus as Messiah and then went on to live a lifestyle that largely **conformed** to the lifestyle Jesus laid out for His followers in the Sermon on the Mount. Living separated lives they lived in communities in which they:

- Lived as resident aliens and pacifists.
- Cared for one another.

- Took care of widows and orphans, and the poor.
- They were persecuted by the world and hated because **they remained faithful to God and their Torah.**
- On the other hand, the Christians, who professed to accept Jesus as Messiah, lived like Gentiles and persecuted the Jews.

The point being here that the Jews are living proof that it is possible to be the kind of community that Jesus founded and commanded His disciples to be. The Jews lived for two thousand years (from the sixth century BC exile to the twentieth century AD) surrounded by pagans but never losing their faith, their identity and their hope. They mixed with the nations in some ways but maintained visible differences as well. We need to learn from the Jews the secrets of surviving in a pagan environment without becoming completely isolated, yet without losing our identity.[4]

Therefore, it is of supreme importance that we in "the faith" realize the relationship between Christ and the Bible, and the relationship of each Christian to the Bible. **Christians must remain faithful to Christ and the Bible.** Many passages in the Bible declare itself to be the "Word of God"—also many passages give the title "the Word" or "the Word of God" to Christ. Notice:

- "In the beginning was the Word, and the Word was with God and the Word was God" (John 1:1).
- He [Christ] was clothed with a robe dipped in blood, and His name is called, "The Word of God" (see Revelation 19:13).

The Bible is the Word of God and Christ is the Word of God, notice:

- Both are divine, authoritative perfect revelation of God.
- Both agree one with the other perfectly.
- Christ perfectly fulfills the Bible.
- The Bible is the Written Word of God and Christ is the Living Word of God.

- Christ was the eternal Word with the Father before His incarnation and He is the Word made flesh in His incarnation.
- The Holy Spirit reveals God through His Word and also in the Word made flesh, Jesus Christ. If Christians are going to survive the increasing persecution and rejection of the main stream and culture, the above statement must be internalized and made a reality.

The point is, if Christ is perfectly one with the Bible—then it's obvious that the relationship of the Christian to the Bible must be the same as his or her relationship to Christ. Abiding in the Word is essential in order to have:

- A proper relationship with Christ.
- To have communion with Christ today, (as we shall see in the next section).

A New kind of Relationship

In John 14, Jesus warns His disciples that soon He in bodily presence would be leaving them; which would require a new kind of relationship between them. Though He will be away from them, they will still be able to see Him. He told them, "A little while longer and the world will see Me no more, but you will see Me" (v. 19). One of the disciples asked, "Lord how is it that you will **manifest Yourself** to us, and not to the world?" (v. 22).

Jesus answered, "If anyone loves Me, he will keep My **Word;** and My Father will love him, and we will come to him and make our home with him" (v. 23). The phrase **"he will keep My Word"** explains clearly the difference between a true Christian and an unbeliever. A true born again Christian keeps or abides in Christ's Word. In his exposition of verse 23, Derek Prince point out four important facts for anyone desiring to become a Christian:

- Keeping God's Word is the supreme feature that distinguishes the true Christian from the world. *This means we should "meditate day and night"* (Psalm 1:2). *We should love and feast upon it every hour [24-7]. Even in our daily occupations, keep the Word of Truth ever before your eyes. [Italics are mine throughout].*

- Keeping God's Word is the test of the Christian's love for God and the major cause of God's favor toward him or her. *We must have the faith that will keep on believing no matter how radical the fluctuation in our emotional state may be.*

- Christ **manifests Himself** to the true Christian through God's Word, as it is applied and obeyed. *This manifestation Of Christ is not a special deluxe edition of Christianity to be enjoyed by a certain few who just happen to be made of finer stuff than the rest of us. Rather, it is the normal state for every true Christian man and woman, girl and boy the world over. It is:*

> *"The mystery which has been hidden*
> *From ages and from generation,*
> *But now*
> *Has been revealed to His saints*
> *What are the riches of the glory*
> *Of this mystery among the Gentiles:*
> *which is*
> *Christ **in you** the hope of glory"*
> (Colossians 1:26-27).

- The Father, the Son, and the Holy Spirit come into the life of the Christian and establish their home with him or her through the Word of God.[5] *We must keep our thoughts a clean sanctuary for their holy habitation.*

Jesus said on occasion, *"Without Me [the Word] you will do anything."* [Bracket is mine]. Note a few of David's observations concerning the importance of abiding in the Word:

- David said, "Your Word have I hid in my heart, that I might not sin against you" (Psalm 119:11). Then in Psalm 101:3, He said, "I will set nothing wicked before my eyes."
- He describes God's Word as **light** that is a **guide for living;** the light also refers to **understanding** (see Psalm 119:103, 130).
- He expresses his love for the Word because **it breathes new life into his soul** (see Psalm 119:132).
- He expresses love for God's Word because **it revives or transforms his life with a new spirit** (see Psalm 119:149).
- He expresses great love for God's Word because **it led him to wisdom and righteousness** (see Psalm 119:97-176).

In the New Testament, the Apostle Paul expresses praise for God's Word because it **pointed out his sin,** and made him realize his desperate **need** for a **Savior** (see Romans 7:7). It has been said, the Word of God is shallow enough for a child to wade in and yet, it is deep enough to drown an adult. The few verses above reflect that there is no life for the Christian without the Word of God. Note the strength and vitality of the phrases from the few passages above:

- It lights your path.
- It guides your living.
- It gives you understanding.
- It helps you to find your way.
- It breathes new life into your soul.
- It receives you.
- It transforms your life.
- It leads you to wisdom and righteousness.
- It shows a person the need for a Savior.

Whenever a need arises in the life of a Christian; there are three actions that he or she should take:

- Ask for the Holy Spirit's guidance to the appropriate promise (s) that apply to the situation and meets your need.

- Obediently take applicable life action(s) on particular requirements attached to the promises.
- Rejoice and positively expect the fulfillment of the promise(s).

For every need that arises in the Christian's life, somewhere in the Word of God is a Promise (s) that will meet that need and it may be claimed through faith in Jesus Christ (see Philippians 4:19). This kind of faith is activated by your action, and victory lies in knowing and applying the promises of God's Word. John said, "This kind of faith overcomes the world" (see 1 John 5:4). Listen as Peter exhorts that same truth. "As His divine power has given to us all things that pertain to life and godliness, through the **knowledge of Him** who called us by virtue and glory by which have been given to us exceedingly great and precious, promises that through these you may be partakers of the **divine nature** having escaped the corruption that is in the world through lust" (2 Peter 1:3-4).

Spiritual Ignorance

Some of America's sharpest minds are in all levels of leadership in all professions including ministry across this country. Yet, we continue to go with the flow of the public culture right or wrong. With the acceptance of **moral relativism,** all of our founding institutions including marriage and family, education at all levels, government at all echelons, and all of our founding documents, along with the Bible are under open attack.

Today our culture has lost the confidence that statements of fact can ever be anything more than just opinions; we no longer know that anything is certain beyond our subjective preferences. The word **truth** now means *"true for me"* and nothing more. We have entered an era of **dogmatic skepticism.**[6]

By means of *repetition* and **passive** *acceptance* over time, they take on the force of common wisdom, a "truth" that everyone knows but no one has stopped to examine, a kind of intellectual legend.[7] Now that these ideas have been part of this generations' educational indoctrination and have **taken root,** they are difficult to dislodge. In fact, much damage has already been done in the church. Pluralism has no doubt always been present in the church, but the situation we face today as Christian leaders and teachers is multifaceted. Those Christians relying on science and reason are already defeated. Only a biblical worldview has a chance in these last days (see Acts 1:8; John 14:25, 26). I don't think pastors and other church leaders are really keeping abreast of what is happening in this country:

- Many churches are hiring people in such positions as minister of music and counselors who hold very prestigious degrees, but are not born again Christians.
- Satan is relying on the spiritual ignorance operating in churches which oppose the things of the Spirit; therefore leaving only the "flesh" or old nature for interpretation of the truth of God's Word and service.
- Some leaders have accepted Christ, but have not received the baptism of the Holy Spirit which would put the supernatural anointing upon every aspect of their being and kingdom service to include wisdom, unity, guidance, and revelation of Truth (see John 14:6). Satan is exploiting and destroying the American church through a lack of spiritual knowledge (see Hosea 4:6).
- Morality now reduced to personal tastes, the question in society is no longer, what **is good?** For the *pleasure question,* what **feels good?** People put forth their desires and then use moral language to try to rationalize their choices.

Our culture is at a place where instead of morality constraining pleasures ("I want to do that, but I really shouldn't")—the pleasures define morality ("I want to do that, and I'm going to **find a way** to rationalize it"). Ethical decisions making in reality is simple self-interests or pleasure as ethics. When self-interest rules, it has a profound impact on **behavior**—especially how we treat other human beings. Human respect and dignity is the existence of moral truth. Otherwise there is no obligation of self-sacrifice for others. Therefore, we can discard people when they become troublesome, expensive or cramp our lifestyle.[8] This type of attitude should not be found among Christians, but it's sad to say, in this area many Christians behave similar to unbelievers in the culture operating through their sin natures.

Where there is no truth, nothing has transcendent value, including the human body. The death of morality reduces people to the status of mere creatures. Without internalizing the truths of God's Word many Christians are reduced as such, because when persons are viewed as things, they begin to be treated as things. I read an article in the paper the other day about a mother who threw her newborn in the sewer. The baby was found some 16 hours later when someone reported hearing what they though was a trapped kitten. The umbilical cord was still attached. The mother's explanation was she couldn't afford to support the child. People are in churches today nurturing a smorgasbord of beliefs a little from this group and a little from that one, at the same time discarding any Bible truth that does not line up with their personal belief; this is similar to the church of the last days found in Revelation 3, the church of the Laodeceans [the peoples' church]. God forbid! The world preaches daily that they have a right to do with their body as they please. God's moral law still stands!

In 1 Corinthians 6:19-20, the Apostle Paul asks, "do you not know that your body is the temple of the Holy Spirit **who is in you,** whom you have from God, and you are not you own?' You were bought for a price; therefore **glorify God** in your body and in your spirit, which are God's." Much has been taught concerning the body which would lead to the belief that your body is your own, evil or unimportant to the salvation process. The Scripture informs concerning the Christians' bodies:

- Your body is a member of Christ (1 Corinthians 6:15).
- Your body is for the Lord (see 1 Corinthians 6:13).

- Your body cost the precious blood of Jesus (see 1 Corinthians 6:20; 1 Peter 1:18).
- Your body is a part of the body of Christ, the church (see 1 Corinthians 6:15; Ephesians 1:22, 23).

Satan is attempting to destroy God's people through the denial of authentic truth and spiritual ignorance concerning sexual sin. God said in His Word, **"My people are destroyed for lack of knowledge"** (Hosea 4:6).

Abide in Christ (Prayers answered)

Jesus exhorted the disciples to abide in Him (John 15:4-5). In verse 6 He warned them of the consequences of **failing to abide.** Now in verse 7 He goes back to the blessings that will be theirs if they **obey His Word:** *"You shall ask what you desire, and it will be done for you."* The abiding Christian has a divine guarantee that God will answer his or her prayers. *I have added emphasis.*

Some people have a misconception and think this means a new home, money, or other material goods and expect God to grant such a request. In fact many charlatans are teaching and preaching today that that is exactly what God will do for them. The abiding Christian will not pray such foolish and selfish prayers; he or she will pray according to His will. 1 John 5:14 promises, *"This is the confidence that we have in Him, that if we ask any thing according to His will, He hears us."* As Christians, we can know with absolute confidence that God answers prayer when we approach the throne of grace according to His will (see Hebrews 4:16). In I John 2:21-22, John assure every Christian, if our hearts do not condemn us, we have confidence toward God. And whatever we ask we receive from Him, because *we keep His commandments and do those things that are pleasing in His sight.*

Abiding in Christ requires full surrender of spirit, soul and body. Such a person maintains heart-communion with our Lord and Savior, Jesus Christ at all times. The, abiding Christian must:

- Continually feed upon the Scriptures.
- Continually pursue a deep desire to know God's Word.
- Continually claim the promises.
- Continually praying in the Spirit according to the will of God.

Keep in you heart, Christ's instructions as found in His Word concerning prayer. Jesus said, "And when you pray:

- You shall not be like the hypocrites. For they love to pray standing in the synagogues and on the corners of the streets, that they may be seen of men. Assuredly, I say to you, they have their reward.
- But you, when you pray, go into you room, and when you have shut your door, pray to your Father who is in the secret place; and your Father who sees in secret will reward you openly.
- Do not use vain repetitions as the heathen do. For they think that they will be heard for their many words.
- Therefore, do not be like them. Your Father knows the things you have need of before you ask Him" (see Matthew 6:5-8).

Abide not in Christ (Hypocrisy)

On an occasion while Jesus was addressing a group of Pharisees concerning the superiority of God's law over man-made traditions and the difference between ceremonial and true moral defilement. He entered the argument by calling the Pharisees hypocrites. The term *"hypocrite"* refers to actors who wear masks on stage as they play different characters. Thus the Pharisees were not genuinely religious; they were simply playing a part for outside show.

Problems in life stem from an unworthy desire in the heart of some person somewhere. In Jeremiah 17:9 we are told, "The heart is deceitful above all things, and desperately wicked: Who can know it?" We must remember that the human heart is our inheritance as members of the Adam's family; therefore, unless the Holy Spirit gives us new life in our spirit and a new nature which places us in Christ; whatever comes out of our minds, emotions, and wills at best will be hypocritical sin-distorted by our inherited sinful nature.

Hypocrisy has become the norm, consuming many Christians and even some whole churches are caught in the sin of hypocrisy; while at the same time claiming to share in Christ and His righteousness. These people involve themselves in religious activity and forms that many times appear to outdo the authentic committed Christians; and this may make it the worst of all heart problems, because it is a lie within their hearts. This sin has an attractive cover to hide the truth. It is not uncommon to see churches employing or assigning individuals to key positions who are known hypocrites, carnal, and in some cases not saved at all. Many times the motive may be to retain the status quo, finances or any number of reasons other than the right one.

Picture if you will the hypocrite of hypocrites, Judas Iscariot displaying all confidence sat with Jesus and the other apostles at Passover as if he was the holiest and most welcomed guest; yet in his evil heart, he had already betrayed Christ.

A person with a divided heart has always posed a problem to them self and the Christian community because they are dominated by their old sinful nature. One part wants to please God, but the other part wants to do its own thing. To better understand this situation, (study Romans 7). A truly righteous person who is growing in grace and the knowledge of our Lord and Savior, Jesus Christ experiences a significant loss of self as they depend totally upon the Holy Spirit to form his or her new nature. (Study Romans 8). An abiding heart for the Lord is willing to reveal sin and face the truth of its ultimate consequences.

As the Holy Spirit forms our new nature in the likeness of Christ, our old nature is dead, however our mind has to be reprogrammed to the new you—totally controlled by the Spirit-formed new nature. Psalm 86:11 is one of the best definitions of a righteous heart. It states, "Teach me your way, O Lord, I will walk in Your truth; and unite my heart to fear Your name." Hide His Word in your heart that you may not sin against Him. Live for His glory.

STUDY GUIDE: CHAPTER 4

THE ABIDING WORD

1. The Holy Spirit forms our new nature into the _____

   _____.

2. What does Christ promise the believer who abides in Him?

3. The Bible is the _____ and Christ is the

   _____.

4. Keeping God's Word is the test of the Christian's
   _____ for _____ and the major cause of
   _____ toward him or her.

5. List three of David's observations concerning the importance of
   abiding in the Word.

   1.

   2.

   3.

6. God said in His Word, "My people are destroyed for a lack of

   _____.

SECTION 2

WHAT GOD REQUIRES

Chapter 5

THE SPIRIT FILLED CHURCH

"Contend for the faith, once delivered to the saints"
(Jude 3)

In an age of relativism, in which there appears to be no absolutes, it is imperative to know first of all that God is still on His throne and He has absolutes. God, His Word, His truth, and His laws stand out as eternal absolutes, time-tested and unchanged. Many philosophies including humanism, relativism, atheism, agnosticism, and multiculturalism [with its multi-religions] have saturated this generation causing a real need for sound doctrine. All of this is happening in a day of a fierce and all-points attack on the American church and God's people in general.

Compounding the problem, are the many churches who claim to have no time for doctrinal preaching or teaching. They have turned to motivation speakers, entertainment, politics, ethics, prosperity, social issues, or a passage of Scripture, twisted to fit specific lifestyles. Many are saying that doctrine is useless and obsolete. Some of their objections:

- Jesus and the apostles formulated their practices as they moved about.
- The church does not need doctrine, because it is divisive and not inclusive.
- What matters is who you believe, not what you believe.
- Doctrinal preaching and teaching is so dull, dead, and useless today.

Those raising these objections resemble someone trying to build a house without first constructing a solid foundation upon which the house is to be anchored. This attitude has almost completely concealed the foundational mandates Christ gave His disciples upon which to build His church.

Why do we need Doctrine?

Doctrine means something taught, teachings, instructions; here it refers to the truths of God's Word that are to be taught. One of these is in Acts 2:42 where the early church *converts* continued steadfastly in the apostles' doctrine. The apostles' doctrine provided the *foundational* content for the believer's spiritual growth and maturity. Charles Swindoll observed, "When the people heard the good news about Jesus, they received "Peter's message. They recognized the truth of God's Word and believed it."[9] In verse 41, the Scripture says, about three thousand souls were added.

Swindoll continues, in spite numbers there was still simplicity. Notice, there was no tradition, there were no church constitution and bylaws, no programs, no senior pastor, no elders board. He further states, *"Instead, we see 3,120 people living their lives with the Spirit of God now living **within** them and **directing** their steps. "*[10] [Emphasis mine] He observes four essentials far a church to be the kind of church Jesus promised to build. In verse 42 they continually devoted themselves to:[11]

- Teaching—foundational and spiritual growth to maturity (see John 14:26; 15:26, 27; 16:13).
- Fellowship—now partners with Jesus Christ and all other believers (see 1 John 1:3).
- Breaking of bread—refers to the Lord's Table or Communion, which is mandatory for all Christians to observe (see 1 Corinthians 11:24-29).
- Prayer—individual Christians and corporately (see 1:14, 24).

These believers though not flawless were empowered of the Holy Spirit as He worked forming their new nature inside, and controlling their lives:

> *So continuing daily with one accord in the temple, and breaking bread from house to house, they ate their food with gladness and simplicity of heart, praising God and having favor with all the people. And the Lord added to the church daily those who were being saved.*
>
> (Acts 2:46-47)

The Jerusalem church was a joyful, Spirit-filled church because its single focus was on Jesus Christ. Salvation is God's *sovereign* work. Amen to that!

> *Then the churches throughout all Judea, Galilee, and Samaria had peace and were edified. And walking in the fear of the Lord and in the comfort of the Holy Spirit, they were multiplied.*
>
> (Acts 9:31)

> *And the hand of the Lord was with them, and a great number believed and turned to the Lord. Then news of these things came to the ears of the church in Jerusalem, and they sent out Barnabas to go to Antioch. When he came and had seen the grace of God, he was glad, and encouraged them all that with purpose of heart they should continue with the Lord. He was a good man, full of the Holy Spirit and of faith. And a great many people were added to the Lord.*

Again, notice the church is [now] in Antioch [Gentile church] and the growth is phenomenal! In spite of intense opposition and persecution and sometimes because of it—Christ continued to build His church. Satan could not stop it!

"I am not ashamed of the gospel of Jesus Christ, for it is the power of God to salvation for everyone who believes, for the Jew first and also for the Greek" (Romans 1:16).

The Power of Words

Ministering is to render priestly service. The Apostle Paul sees himself as a priest offering a sacrifice to God. The sacrifice is the Gentile believers who have been made acceptable to God, through, "their obedience to the Word (see Romans 15:17-18).

This is not of his own, but in Christ that he does it. Paul was a worker of miracles, but only by the power of the Holy Spirit. He took no credit for anything Christ accomplished through him.

His ministry was very effective. He impacted great cities full of paganism, and planted strong churches. The Thessalonians serves as a prime example, they "turned from idols to serve the living God" (I Thessalonians 1:9). He commended them for their faith and reminded them that his gospel had come to them not in Word only, but in power and in the Holy Spirit (I Thessalonians 1:5). There seems to be two schools of thought concerning the Holy Spirit's presence:

- One says that this is a private and personal experience which shouldn't have any connection with your going to church.
- The second is that without the Holy Spirit any attempt at worship or any service for God personal or corporate would be natural, in the flesh which is what the human spirit is without the Holy Spirit.

By that formula of the power of the Holy Spirit and the Word, the disciples were said to have turned the world upside down. The gospel in word and power! It is imperative that these same ingredients are present in our preaching and teaching today.

Therefore when the church is gathered the presence of the Holy Spirit is meant to be evident; if we are the Spirit-filled community we can't miss Him. The Scripture says that the manifestation of the Spirit is for the common good (see 1 Corinthians 10:8). Therefore, the manifest presence of the Holy Spirit is non-negotiable! Paul defines the true people of God as those **"who worship God in the Spirit, rejoice in Christ Jesus, and have no confidence in the flesh"** (Philippians 3:3).

The gospel comes in word, and must be understood. In His parable of the seed, Jesus pointed out that the word received must be understood. The Scripture says, "The Word of God is **living** and **powerful,** and **sharper** than any two-edged sword, piercing even to the division of soul and spirit, and joints and marrow, and is a discerner of the thoughts and intents of the heart" (Hebrews 4:12). The Word of God is the measuring rod Christ will use in the judgment (see 2 Corinthians 5:10). God's Word is alive and active, penetrating the innermost parts of a person, it distinguishes:

- What is natural and what is spiritual.
- The thoughts and intents of a person.
- The Word of God exposes the natural and spiritual motivations of a believer's heart.

Seriously study the following passages (Hebrews 4:7; 3:8, 10, 12, 15; 8:10; 10:16, 22; 13:9).[12] The Thessalonians received the word "not as the word of men, but for what it really is, the Word of God. Phillip's first question to the Ethiopian was, "Do you understand?" Clear biblical factors rooted in the presence of the Holy Spirit are missing in so many of our churches. There is a great need for restoration in the church, not just personal renewal or even revival—but some organizational and structural issues have got to be addressed and changed; so that the Holy Spirit can take His rightful place.

First Things First

Many of the people coming into the church today want to bring their own personal ideas about God and life. Even when hearing the biblical Christian message, many prefer to continue their traditional practices and retaining their independent knowledge no matter what God has revealed in His Word. Human perceptions of God and His requirements fall far short of God's revelation. The foundation of all true knowledge of God must be a clear mental apprehension of His perfections as revealed in the Scripture.

People not only come into the church with their own preconceived views of God, but the sad fact is many within the church develop their own concepts of error after collecting a little here and a little there. We hear, "My God and I" or "God is love and will save everybody." Like Paul, we must preach a message not in the wisdom of men, but in demonstration of the Spirit and power, so that faith won't rest on the wisdom of men, but on the power of God (see 1 Corinthians 2:4-5). Jesus said it, "Except a man be born again he cannot see the kingdom of Heaven.

Much of the confusion experienced in churches could be prevented if we would turn back to God's Word and rely on the Holy Spirit for wisdom and understanding. James explained, "For as the body without the Spirit is dead, so faith without works is dead" (see James 2:26).

Be Transformed

The Word of God transforms you by renewing your mind or in other words changes your thinking. The Scripture says, "As a man thinks in his heart so is he" (Proverbs 23:7). In conversion when the Holy Spirit quickens the sinner in salvation, he or she becomes a new creature in Christ (see 2 Corinthians 5:21), we are the righteousness of God. All things become new. Because we were born in sin and shaped in iniquity, our nature was sinful. A dogs nature is to bark and a cat's nature is to meow, but the nature [called the old man] of man is to sin.

While our old nature is gone [dead] it has left a body (see Romans 6:6). Similarly, when we die our spirit returns to God if we are saved and Sheol if we are unsaved. At any rate we all leave a body. At that point we have the mind of Christ, and we must think like Him and act like Him. You must now see yourself as a new person.

The old "self" body of sin must be destroyed; this is accomplished by renewing your mind as we are being transformed through the truths of God's Word. This body of sin refers to sinful propensities that are intertwined memories of our old sinful ways and other weaknesses (see Romans 8:10, 11, 13, 23). Although the old self is dead, sin still has a foothold in our unredeemed humanness and its corrupt desires (see 7:14-24). Everything we need to become a mature believer in Christ has been divinely given to us. We must walk by faith, not by sight. We have believed in Christ unto salvation, practice walking in it. Many times on my way home I pass certain landmarks, but don't remember going by them. Practice righteousness and sooner or later that old body of sin will be less than a memory. The intensity of the fight will be determined by your love for Christ coupled with your will becoming His will. Christ has freed us. However, that does not mean that all will accept that freedom. Once the Israelites were set free to return to Jerusalem, many remained in Babylon. A renewed mind will counter the old man thinking. The Word of God is the sword of the Spirit which we raise up against the wiles of the devil. Jesus demonstrated how this is done as He dealt with the devil (see Matthew 4:1-11). To be successful in this battle, you must develop some personal holy habits to keep you sharp and sustain you through the battle:

- Personal and corporate Bible study.
- Continuously memorizing and meditating on the Word.
- Prayer [personal and corporate].

Much prayer—much power and little prayer—little power

Many cultures with less facilities and resources than we have here in America are gladly embracing the supernatural elements of the gospel. My wife and I witnessed this fact in the Far East and Central and South America. I believe that we are going to be less concerned in this country with our traditions, and buildings, this will be forced by the exodus from the pews. I warn constantly in my teaching that pastors must lead their churches into the supernatural realm because we are going to be persecuted sooner than we think. A Spirit-filled church will stand if we follow closely the model of the early church. It is imperative that we pass our faith on to our children and their children.

The Churches' Challenge [Multiculturalism]

Every day our nation becomes more secularized. In the past Christian leaders were consulted and readily engaged the culture, however, with the rejection of biblical Christianity due to its exclusivity, more and more local churches today seem to be in full retreat and energized with their great programs, musical performances, and other attractions. We are called like the early church was to live out our faith in the midst of a lost world, representing Christ to unbelievers everywhere. The U.S. government and courts have become more secularized, and society has displayed open rejection and hostility toward Christians and Christianity. Through multicultural indoctrinations in the schools, our children will be more familiar with Islam or the New Age religions than their founding faith, biblical Christianity. All of this poses a greater challenge to the church for years to come.

From coast to coast the multicultural experiences are the same—stretching their view of God. Multicultural education teaches tolerance, respect, and appreciation for the worlds diverse cultures, belief systems, and lifestyles. It accepts religions because they are inclusive and rejects Christianity because it is exclusive [Jesus said, "**Except** you are born again, you can not see the kingdom of God," see John 3:3. Some thirteen years into the new century, the fruit of this shift in paradigm is reflected in the mosaics, 18-29 years olds, and the first wave of our global children moving into leadership positions in our churches and society. One out of every four young adults (27 percent) stated that they "grew up a Christian, but they perceive that the church has kept them fearful and detached from the world. They look for excitement outside traditional boundaries. This may be pornography or sexual experimentation, drugs, internet, and extreme thrill seeking. Additionally they have tried other faiths or spiritual practices."[13]

Having rejected biblical Christianity the education change agents realized that some kind of global spirituality was needed to fuel a collective pursuit of global unity. It seems that any of the world's New Age and neopagan religions would do except Christianity. Offering a common alternative to the biblical God, they all **blend** one or more of the following:

- **Pantheism:** All is God and God is all, since a universal force infuses all things with spiritual life. Today's popularized versions encourages everyone to "look within: for the strength, wisdom, and guidance needed to empower oneself for success.
- **Monism:** All is one, joined together through the pantheistic spirituality.
- **Polytheism:** Many gods. Since the pantheistic deity makes everything sacred, people can worship anything or anyone they choose. Children learn that in the end, all the world's gods lead to the same happy spirit world.

Oneness is the heartbeat of global spirituality. I believe that pluralism causes many casualties among the 18-29 years old groups. Many even after significant exposure to biblical Christianity as children, teenagers and young adults are missing from the pews and active commitment to Christ. Statistics show that, of those churches effectively reaching these young people, the number reached is only a drop in the bucket, considering the number of young people who reside in their local community. Generations of young people in the past left the church, but after marriage, entering a career or at some point returned. This generation is not returning.

Another challenge presented by multiculturalism is Islam. My wife and I along with some family members traveled from North Carolina to Boston, Massachusetts for a family retreat. An unusual number of the hotels, gas stations and convenient stores were manned by Muslims along the way up and back. Later on a trip to St. Petersburg, Florida we ran into the same accommodations. I suspect traveling west we would find the same. Statistically there are seven million Muslims in America. That's about the population of New York City; however, they are all over this country in cities, towns and villages alike. If there is an agenda to spread Islam throughout this country as found in Europe; the people are certainly being put into position for such a move with what seems to be most favored status in politics. Europe has forfeited any right to criticize Islam. America is increasingly following in their footsteps as they totally ignore all of the signals. At the same time authentic Christianity is being rejected as judgmental, bigoted and obsolete. In Islamic countries Christians are often put to death for dishonoring Islam. Islam is not just a religion; it is a political ideology. Periodically, the media reports incidents wherein and individual or family personally invokes Sharia law to handle a family dispute usually ending in death. A cursory examination reveals that Sharia is totally incompatible with democracy and human rights.[14] In roads are subtly being made for instance crosses being removed from hospitals and churches so as to not offend Muslims. Additionally a so-called insider movement is growing in this country. Often introduced in two ways:

- Some describe them as missionary methods of contextualizing the gospel for Muslims.
- It is thought of as "church planting" in a Muslim context.

People quietly claim Jesus as Lord from within their identities as Muslims. They neither "convert" nor turn from their previous religions. As the theory goes, a person claims Jesus as Lord and then becomes a religious dual citizen, *Chrislam,* maintaining spiritual passports as Muslim and also as a follower of Jesus.[15] The question is which Jesus are you going to follow?

Rather than fanning flames of hatred for Muslims, New Agers or any communities, we should view them with forgiveness and much grace. We have our mandate to go throughout the whole world with the gospel of Christ; thoroughly prepared to give a reason for our stand for the truth of God's Word. We must have a burden for America all of America, as pastors and teachers we must educate our congregations now so that as Spirit-filled biblical Christians they will be prepared to make the proper choices and decisions; and remaining faithful and loyal in sharing the gospel our Lord and Savior, Jesus Christ. As we all see that day coming be prepared to suffer for the cause of Christ as the need approaches. Lord I pray that as we face the challenges facing the church may we be ever mindful that we are mere moons reflecting the Son of God. To Him be glory and honor forever.

STUDY GUIDE: CHAPTER 5

THE SPIRIT-FILLED CHURCH

1. Doctrine means something taught or _____.

2. How did Paul describe the gospel of salvation?

3. Explain (below) the two schools of thought concerning the Holy Spirit's presence.

4. In what way or ways does multiculturalism affect Christianity in America?

5. Explain (below) the culture's attitude toward Christianity,

6. Explain (below) Islam's insider movement in this country.

7. How is pluralism affecting the 18-29 year olds in America?

Chapter 6

REMEMBER WHO YOU ARE

I came across some old high school photos the other day which I had taken back in 1958. The gloss had faded some but I could recognize everyone in the picture. I thought about the process then and now, technically advanced but the same principle. Point the camera at your subject, press the shutter button and the light will burn and impression of your subject, much of what we use to concern ourselves with proper lighting, holding the camera still is still there and the finished product is a record of your memories.

God has taken six pictures of the church in order to give you a clearer understanding how you are to relate to each picture. God has pointed His camera at the church, pressed the shutter, and His light has burned an impression. His work completed, He offers six pictures of the church. Ephesians 2:19-22 presents God's work in six authentic impressions: a New Nation, God's family, God's building, a Growing Organism, a Worldwide Temple and a Local Temple:

Picture #1—A New Nation (v. 19)

Over the two thousand years since Christ died for our sins and rose from the grave, the sharp edge of the gospel message has been dulled through rationalization and unbelief. As a result it seems that everyone have their own perceptive theology concerning the truths of God's word. One says, "All ways lead to God," another says, "God loves us too much to let anyone go to hell." However, God's Word leaves no doubt from God perspective.

There was a time when we were as a stranger or foreigner to God, when we were not citizens of God's kingdom. We had no relationship and no fellowship with God and no home and no rights to citizenship in His kingdom. But praises be to God, we are no longer strangers and foreigners to God. Jesus Christ has brought us to God. The man Adam lost or forfeited dominion to Satan, but Jesus Christ came and took it back. God's kingdom is made up of the people from all the ages that have trusted in Him. There are no strangers, foreigners, or second-class citizens there (see Philippians 3:20).

Paul sets out in Romans 5:12-21 to show how one man's death provides salvation for many. To prove his point, he uses Adam to establish the principle that it is possible for one man's actions to inexorably affect many other people:

> *"Therefore, just as through one man sin, entered the world, and death through sin, and thus death spread to all men, because all sinned—(For until the law sin was in the world, but sin is not imputed when there is no law. Nevertheless death reigned from Adam to Moses, even over those who had not sinned according to the likeness of the transgression of Adam, who was a type of Him who was to come. But the free gift is not like the offense. For if by the one man's offense many died, much more the grace of God and the gift by the grace of the one Man, Jesus Christ, abounded to many. And the gift is not like that which came through the one who sinned. For the judgment which came from one offense resulted in condemnation, but the free gift which came from many offenses resulted in justification. For if by the one man's offense death reigned through the one, much more those who receive abundance of grace and of the gift of righteousness will reign in life through the One, Jesus Christ. Therefore, as through one man's offense judgment came to all men, resulting in condemnation, even so through one Man's righteous act the free gift came to all men, resulting in justification of life. For as by one man's*

disobedience many were made sinners, so also by one Man's obedience many will be made righteous. Moreover the law entered that the offense might abound. But where sin abounded grace abounded much more, so that as sin reigned in death, even so grace might reign through righteousness to eternal life through Jesus Christ our Lord."

Paul further clarifies, *"Being justified freely by His grace through the redemption that is in Christ Jesus, whom God set forth as a propitiation **by His blood, through faith** . . . ."* (Romans 3:24).

We are now biblical Christians and no longer strangers and foreigners to God, because of Jesus Christ who shed His life's blood for us; we are now fellow heavenly citizens with all of God's people. We are saints, a people set apart to God—a *new* people being built into a new nation under God.[16]

Picture #2—God's Family (v. 19)

Jesus Christ has brought us into the family of God. We have been adopted as children of God, sons and daughters of His, and all experiences of God's family are now ours; that includes the privilege of responsibility and service. The Scriptures assure us,

> *"For you did not receive the spirit of bondage again, to fear, but you received the Spirit of adoption by whom we cry out, "Abba Father." The Spirit Himself bears witness with our spirit that we are children of God, and if children, then heirs—eirs of God and joint heirs with Christ, if indeed we suffer with Him, that we may also be glorified together"*

> (Romans 8:15-17).

Hopefully, some of us remember our old daily household chores. Every person of the house hold had duties to perform, some service to render for the sake of the family. The same holds true for God's family. We are responsible to love and care, provide and teach each other. It is also our responsibility of service to build up and strengthen the family of God. The Scripture says,

> *"As we have therefore opportunity, let us do good unto all men, especially unto them who are of the household of faith"*
>
> (Galatians 6:10).

God seeks those who are willing to serve with an excellent spirit.— without having to be asked. He has already told us what to do and provided the tools, the strength, and all the resources we need to serve Him. It's up to us to be obedient in our service.

Picture #3—God's Building (v. 20)

Biblical Christians are pictured as being the building stones which are being used to construct a building for God. Notice two specific points:

1. Jesus Christ Himself is the *chief cornerstone.*

    *   *The cornerstone is the first one laid.* All other stones are placed after it. It is the preeminent stone in time. So it is with Christ. He is the first of God's new movement. Christ is the captain of our salvation; the author of eternal salvation and of our faith. (Study Hebrews 2:10; 12:2; Revelation 1:8).
    *   *The cornerstone is the supportive stone.* All other stones are placed upon it and held by it. They all rest upon it. The cornerstone is the preeminent stone in position and power. So it is with Christ. He is the support and power, the foundation of God's new movement. (Study 1 Corinthians 3:11; Ephesians 2:20-22).

- *The cornerstone is the directional stone.* It is used to line up the whole building and all other stones. It can be called the *instructional stone*—upon it all the lines and instructions of the building are based. So it is with Christ. He is the Person who gave the directions and instructions to God's people. We—the church—are to build our lives upon His instructions and His instructions only. If we follow any other instructions or directions we are out of line; and when we are noticed, we will have to be removed, cast aside, and replaced with a stone that can be set in line. Jesus Christ is the chief cornerstone. God used Him to give direction to all the other stones. (Study 1 Peter 2:6-8; Matthew 7:24-27).

Jesus Christ is the chief cornerstone. Many churches are collapsing today, because some have removed Him. So, no Christ—no church! Christ holds *everything within* the church together. Therefore it is absolutely necessary that He and He alone be preached, taught, and lived.[17]

2. We, the church are built upon the foundation:

- Laid by the testimonies of the apostles and prophets.
- Their testimony of the truths of God's Word itself is the foundation upon which the church is to be laid.

God made certain that His foundation was sure by making Jesus Christ the chief cornerstone. Because the cornerstone is in place, every other stone will be in line, and the church will be built the right way.

Picture #4—A Growing Organism (v. 21)

The church is pictured as a living organism—the union of various parts of a living being, of a dynamic body. This may seem strange to speak of a building that grows. More and more believers are brought in and fitted into the building each day. The building grows and grows and is expected to keep growing until the Lord Jesus Christ comes.[18]

Peter calls Jesus Christ the *living stone.* Christ is the living stone upon whom all others are built. All others must be built upon Him if they wish to live and have their spiritual sacrifice accepted by God. (Study 1 Peter 2:4-5).

Notice, it's all of God; it is all due to God's work. He is the One who raises up Jesus, the Savior. The church and its biblical Christians have two dynamic challenges in this point:

- The church must grow. It must be bringing in new stones [biblical Christians] and fitting them into the building of God. The church must be adding on to the building. Its structure is not completed yet.
- Every Christian within the building is a part of the building and expected to fulfill its function within the building; that is, every Christian is a laborer, who is expected to be busy adding on to the building of the church. We are all to be bringing new stones and fitting them into the great building of God, the church. (Study Matthew 28:19-20).

Throughout the history of the church, Satan has also tried to abort or destroy the body of Christ, the church. In spite of his opposition the church will be triumphant. Jesus reminded us of this when He said, ". . . . **upon this rock I will build My church; and the gates of hell shall not prevail against it**" (Matthew 16:18b).

Picture #5—A Worldwide Temple, the Universal Church (v. 21)

All believers make up the holy temple of God. All believers are pictured as a building, a universal church being structured for God's presence. Each new believer and each generation of believers are seen as being placed and fitted into the universal structure. All believers the world over of every generation is being fitted into God's universal building which will literally be the new heaven and earth. However, each person is placed into the structure *only by Christ.* Only the person and the body of people who come to Christ as the chief cornerstone are fitted into the building.

A person must build upon the foundation laid by the apostles and prophets, which is the foundation of Christ Himself. Any other cornerstone or any other foundation constructs some other kind of building such as:

- Some people may follow their own thought structure.
- Some may follow some man or woman's philosophy.
- Some may follow a specific lifestyle.

In Christ alone! The gospel of Jesus Christ is available to all people everywhere. There is no place for division and prejudice. People from the uttermost part of the earth, is to be brought into the universal temple or church of God.

Picture #6—A Local Temple, the Local Church (v. 22)

Here Paul uses the word "you" referring to the Ephesian church in particular. Each local church is pictured as a building structured for God's presence (v. 22). And each member is seen as an essential stone being placed and fitted into the building (Ephesians 4:16; 1 Peter 2:5). The church's stability lies in each stone's being placed, fitted and cemented by the same Lord so that:

- Each new believer is a new stone in Christ's temple.
- Each stone holding up its load.
- Each stone fulfilling its purpose in the structure.

The local church exists for the purpose of providing a habitation, a home for the presence of God—through His Spirit. The church is to allow the Spirit of God to live out His life through the church. The Spirit of God dwells within the church to conform the church to the image of God's will. The effectiveness of any local church depends upon how much it allows the Holy Spirit to dwell within and to control its body of members.[19]

> *"Do you not know that you are the temple of God*
> *and that the Spirit of God dwell in you?"*
> **(1 Corinthians 3:16).**

Now that you have had the opportunity to closely examine God's photos of the church. You saw the church from six different perspectives. If you look closely enough, you should be able to see yourself in each of these pictures. You have a vital role in the development of the church. Are you doing your part in developing the church—in making the church everything it should be?

STUDY GUIDE: CHAPTER 6

REMEMBER WHO YOU ARE

1. Are you in a church that is built upon Jesus? If not, why not?

2. If you are not in the right church are you praying for God to lead you to the right church?

3. What can you do personally to improve the spiritual life in your church?

4. Should we offer to serve or wait to be asked to serve in your church family?

5. Are you comfortable with the fact that people from every nation, tribe and tongue will be in heaven with you? Why or Why not?

6. Name some of the things you've tried to do that failed because of a poor foundation?

7. What happens to a church that does not have a solid foundation built upon Christ?

Chapter 7

THE CHURCH'S HIGHEST PRIORITY

*I, therefore, the prisoner of the Lord, beseech you to walk worthy of the calling with which you were called, with all lowliness and gentleness, with longsuffering, bearing with one another in love, endeavoring to keep **the unity of the Spirit** in the bond of peace.*

(Ephesians 4:1-3).

We desperately need this practical admonition of the apostle. More than ever the church must stand and be the church that Christ died for and rose to empower. To do that Paul says, "Lead a life worthy of the calling to which you have been called (v. 1). The church is called to live counter to the culture in which we find ourselves today. Days have never been so dark in this nation; yet I believe the church is especially called for such a time as this.

Jesus who called us sees much more clearly than we do. He devised a strategy before the world began that will actually remove the *root cause* of the present human darkness that seems to cover this nation and the Western world. Though leadership at national and the local levels have turned their back on God, the church must remain faithful to its Founder and Head, Jesus Christ. When the church is faithful to its calling, it becomes a healing agency for society, able to lift a whole nation to a higher plain of health and wholesome living.

The true church is here to bring that strategy to fruition. The false church is here to oppose it; keep reading and you will see that it was to no avail. But biblical Christians actually promote the *causes* of false Christianity when, through spiritual ignorance or misguided zeal deviate from the divine strategy with their limited human perceptions, disobey their divine calling. We mere humans cannot improve on the plan of God. Nor are we to falter because of the way things may appear—we are left with no doubt of what that calling is. Many passages throughout the New Testament are devoted to describing and detailing it.

Reality

If we would begin by facing reality, it would be apparent that our best human strategies are founded upon limited human understanding and the best estimates of any situation human beings can make are flawed and earthy as a result of Adam's sin. But God's strategy and calling upon our lives, is based upon His absolutely perfect understanding of fundamental and ultimate reality. That is the glory of biblical Christianity because:

- It sets forth things as they really are.
- The Christian diagnosis of all the world's ills—from conflicts between nations to conflicts with worldviews and cultures, to conflicts in the individual soul is accurate because it reflects a true understanding of the human condition.
- The New Testament epistles always begin with the *truth*—which is known as "doctrine." The New Testament writers always call us back to reality. Then, on the basis of that underlying *foundation of the truths of God's Word*, they go on to suggest certain practical applications. Why be foolish and start with anything but truth?

In the three opening chapters of Ephesians, Paul makes several clear purpose statements for the church not just for eternity, but for the here and now. Notice:

1. *The church is to reflect the holiness of God.* (see Ephesians 1:4).

   - God chose us before the foundation of the world.
   - That we should be **holy** and **blameless** in **love.**
   - God's plan and strategy are obviously independent of human influence.

The question may arise, "what is God's first consideration for the church?" Paul is setting forth in this writing that what the church *is* comes before what the church *does.* Understanding the moral character of God's people is essential to understanding the nature of the church.[20]

As biblical Christians we are to be moral examples to the world, reflecting the pure character and holiness of Jesus Christ.

As the moon having no light of its own, reflects the light of the sun—we having no light of our own reflect the light of the Son.

2. *The church is to reveal God's glory* (v. 5).

The first task of the church is not the welfare of humanity, though welfare is important to God. Rather, we have been chosen by God to live to the praise and glory of God, so that through our lives His glory will be *revealed* to the world. As the New English Bible states it, "We should cause His glory to be praised."[21]

3. *The church is to be a witness to Christ* (1 Peter 2:9).

The apostle Peter has a word concerning the church's witnessing role, *"You are a chosen race, a royal priesthood, a holy nation,*

God's own people, that you may declare the wonderful deeds of him who called you out of darkness into his marvelous light."

We are indwelt by Christ so that He may demonstrate His life and character through us. The responsibility to fulfill this calling of the church belongs to every biblical Christian. The expression of the church's witness may sometimes be corporate, but the responsibility to witness to Christ is always individual. It is so easy for the church or the individual Christian to talk about displaying the character of Christ; however, upon close observation the image many Christians display is not the true biblical image of Jesus Christ. Therefore, in (Ephesians 4:2-3), Paul goes on to describe the biblical marks of Christlike character:

- Humility
- Patience
- Love
- Unity
- Peace

The Spirit-bestowed *oneness* of all true Christians has created the bond of peace, the spiritual cord that surrounds and binds God's holy people together. This bond is love. (see Colossians 3:14).

The church must be patient and forbearing, knowing that the truths of God's Word take time to sprout and grow, and time to produce a harvest. The Spirit-filled church is not to demand that society make abrupt changes to long established social patterns. Rather the church is to promote positive social change by shunning evil and practicing righteousness, and then the truths of God's Word will take root in society and bear the fruit of change.

STUDY GUIDE: CHAPTER 7

THE CHURCH'S HIGHEST PRIORITY

- Explain (below) how the church is to live counter to the culture?

- We have two churches in one, how did Jesus address this situation?

- Summarize Peter's comment, that the Christian is to be a witness for Christ.

- List (below) Paul's biblical marks of a Christian.

What is the spiritual bond that holds the church together?

SECTION 3

TRUTH IN CHRISIS

Chapter 8

THE PROMISE OF THE FATHER

"For God has not given us a spirit of fear, but of power and of love and of a sound mind"

(2 Timothy 1:7).

"But you shall be baptized with the Holy Spirit not many days from now"

(Acts 1:5b).

"But you shall receive power when the Holy Spirit has come upon you; and you shall be witnesses to Me in Jerusalem, and in Judea and Samaria, and to the end of the earth"

(Acts 1:8).

Many are questioning today whether the church is relevant. The answer to that question probably depends on who is doing the asking. Some see the church as a country club for antiquated cultural dropouts, for others a dignified place to be entertained, and to some it is just another political action committee.

The church must break through all of this and become the true biblical Christians and church that God intended. In its own collective natural strength, the church is defeated already. This is seen in the confused and frightened faces of so many congregations today. Many are suffering because their denominational parents and grandparents rejected the gracious gift of the Holy Spirit promised by the Father.

Though born again, they were not prepared for the onslaught began back in the sixties wherein all authority including that of the local church was challenged and then gradually rejected by the culture. Instead of turning to the truths of God's Word for guidance, wisdom and strength, many churches turned to denominational theology, how-to-change books and kits based on science and reason; as they lose their identity and purpose.

Yet despite all its weaknesses, hypocrisies, and sin—the church remains the most powerful force on earth for good, from the apostolic times up to the present. It has been a light in the blackest darkness of this world, a paradox? Yes, many of the most precious truths of God's Word come wrapped in a paradox. God created and designed the church to be so.

The natural and the spiritual

How do we unravel this paradox? How can a church reflect both sin and darkness and at the same time reflect light and righteousness? How can it be the source of both spiritual ignorance and spiritual revelation knowledge? We find the answers in the Bible.

In Matthew 13, Jesus uses a number of parables to describe conditions in the world during the period of time between His first and His second coming. *That period of time is the age in which we now live.* One of the parables he told is called the parable of the wheat and the tares or weeds. In the story, Jesus says that He Himself, as the Son of Man, plants wheat in the field of the world. The wheat (good seed) called the "children of the kingdom," represents believers. But after the wheat is planted, the devil comes in and plants weeds or tares. The tares look like wheat but produce no grain. The tares represent counterfeit Christians, whom Jesus calls "sons of the evil one." Outwardly, the counterfeit Christians look like the real thing, just as tares look just like real wheat. The wheat and tares grow up together and look just a like for a while.

One day the workers notice the tares growing among the wheat and ask if they should dig up the tares. The Lord answers, no. Uprooting the tares would destroy the wheat. Instead, "let the wheat and the tares grow together until the harvest" (Matthew 13:30). Jesus concludes the story; the harvest will take place at the close of the age when He sends His angels into the field to separate the tares from the wheat. The tares or weeds will be burned in the judgment, but the wheat will be gathered into the father's barns.

The wheat, true biblical Christians, the sons of the kingdom is those who have experienced the new birth. As Jesus says, "Unless one is born again, he [or she] cannot see the kingdom of God" (John 3:3). The apostle Peter later describes the authentic Christians as being "born anew not of perishable seed but of imperishable, through the living and abiding Word of God" (1 Peter 1:23). The sons of the evil one are the false or counterfeit Christians, never born again by the power of the Holy Spirit of God through faith in the truths of God's Word.

True and False Nature

In God's sight, the false Christians are children of the devil. To some people and even whole churches, the false Christians are indistinguishable from the true Christians. Hopefully now, you see why the church presents such a confusing picture to the world. True and false Christians also mean true and false natures. In reality we have two churches in one community. As the saying goes "oil and water doesn't mix;" neither does true and false. So many local churches are unrecognizable today even as a part of the body of Christ because they have allowed the false Christians, who sometimes think that they are the true, to be the major influence and pace setters in the [life] of the church which has fallen into deception:

- They rejected the promise.
- They have lost their mission and purpose.
- They have created church activities to fill the void left after losing their mission and purpose.
- They succumb to the tares majority.

First of all let me point out, this is not a denominational thing. True Christianity is not about organizations or groups. Neither can we go around with a spiritual magnifying glass trying to detect who is true and who is false. The Bible reveals two truths that must be considered when looking into this matter of true and false Christians:

- It is biblically true that a false or counterfeit Christian can only manifest false or counterfeit Christianity.
- However, true Christians are capable of displaying both true and false Christianity—though not at the same time.

Through spiritual ignorance or willful disobedience true Christians can display a false Christianity in their lives. The sad truth is many Christians today choose to live this self-deceptive and *miserable* life. Having experienced this condition for a while myself, I don't believe there is any sin that can so:

- Grieve the Holy Spirit, who continues to love, convict and woo you back.
- Cause grief, pain and suffering to love ones; and alienate friends.
- Crush your witness to the unsaved world around you, and cause many weak brethren to stumble.
- Brings shame and dishonor to our Lord, who continues to pour love, grace and mercy upon you.

If this is your condition, you need to repent and get back to a right relationship with God, before it is too late. If you are a child of God in this condition; there is never any peace with Him, and therefore you are probably a nervous wreck. Notice the Holy Spirit and Christ are both wooing you to return. Get back in there and fight the good fight!

What is important at this point is your relationship with God; and not those excuses or people whom the devil continually keep before you, to keep you from surrendering all to Jesus. If you are truly saved you are under grace:

- God loves you.
- There is a love one or friend who knows where you are loves you, and is praying for you. Pay attention, God can reach you through them.
- If you are saved you are a partaker of Christ's divine nature. It's there because God put it there and no matter what I know you love the Lord and desire to serve Him. A sinner experiences none of the above.
- You are saved in your spirit, but there is something in your flesh that is hanging on for dear life. Give it up before it takes yours!
- God's Word is a lamp unto our feet and a light unto our path. The gospel is still the power of God unto salvation; which includes deliverance.
- When it is all over you should land in God's will and your destiny.

How did we get there?

First of all immaturity and carnality accepts all ages eight to eighty, also it will accept your family, career, position or whatever you have to offer on the altar of self. Let's face it if you are having a problem with your flesh, then you are not fully grown in your spirit. Until your spirit overcomes your flesh you are yet carnal (see 1 Corinthians 5:1-12). You are not allowing your new nature to Spirit-form you. We will cover the remedy for this condition this more fully in the next chapter.

Today little more than a decade into the twenty-first century I would warn those in church leadership to care for your sheep especially lambs. Twenty or so years ago there were a few true Christians to consider who were caught up in disobedience either because people had convictions or maybe fear. Today however, the false Christians are in the church demanding that they be recognized and claiming a right to their particular lifestyle. This sin shows no remorse and can be found from the pulpit to the door. Counterfeit Christians can only display a counterfeit Christianity. Which church are you referring to?

It is the utmost important today that we study the Scriptures paying careful attention to the Book of Acts and the early church's nature, power and function. We can experience that power today. The world is getting more complex with each passing day. However, the power that turned the world upside down in the book of Acts is available to us. Apathy, biblical and spiritual ignorance is presently hindering the church. By no means do we have to give in to the tares, counterfeit Christians in our churches. For, "Greater is He that is in us then he that is in the world" (1 John 4:4). Like the apostles, we need to instruct Christians about how to recognize the counterfeit Christianity that is among them.

STUDY GUIDE: CHAPTER 8

THE PROMISE OF THE FATHER

1. Summarize (below) the parable of the wheat and the tares.

2. The wheat represents the _____ and the tares represent the _____.

3. A false Christian can only manifest _____ Christianity.

4. A true Christian can manifest _____ and _____ Christianity, but not at the same time.

5. Though the world is growing worse daily; that some power that turned the world upside down is available to the church. What is stopping the church from using that same power?

6. What did the apostle John proclaim in 1 John 4:4?

The gospel is the _____ of God unto _____.

Chapter 9

RECEVING THE PROMISE
OF THE FATHER

"For by one Spirit we were all baptized into one body; whether Jews or Greeks, whether slaves or free; and have all been made to drink into one Spirit"

(1 Corinthians 12:13).

We hear much today reference the baptism of the Holy Spirit; however it is so sad when what is said about Him is error. Many will speak of Him as it, a feeling, to others He is some type of energy, influence or force. Many Christians are cheated of a personal relationship with the Holy Spirit because they have been led somehow to believe one or more of the definitions. Additionally, there are those who teach that the Holy Spirit came on Pentecost, but returned to heaven. Then there are those who believe the Holy Spirit's works of miracles, healing and other supernatural activities ended with the death of the apostles. This confusion has caused many to fear the Holy Spirit and never come to the reality that a viable Christian life is impossible without a relationship with Him. However, the Scriptures say the Holy Spirit is a person and the third person of the Godhead, the Trinity. The Holy Spirit does influence the life of the Christian, and He is revealed as the power of God, but this influence is a personal one—that can "keep you from falling" (see Jude 24).

The Holy Spirit in the life of the true Christians

There are several reasons why this misunderstanding is robbing the church of the truth of God's Word concerning the proper doctrine of the Holy Spirit:

- The Greek word for Spirit is ("Pneuma") and means "breath" or "wind", which implies the concept of an unseen force (see Isaiah 40:7; John 3:5-8).
- The Holy Spirit's work seems to be secret or invisible. However, that does not deny the personality of the Spirit, the Scripture says, *"God is a Spirit"* (John 4:24) and yet He is a divine Person.
- People have little difficulty relating the title "Father" and "Son", but relating to the Holy Spirit as a title is much more difficult (see Matthew 28:19).

When Christians consider the Holy Spirit as a mere influence, feeling, or impersonal force, the results are counter to the truth:

- It is error and contrary to the teaching of Bible truth.
- It hinders worship.
- It will block proper reverence.
- It will prevent a personal relationship.

These misconceptions can cause a person to look upon the Holy Spirit as something like "power" and want to buy it. See the example of Simon the Sorcerer in Acts 8:9-24. The true Christian has more than a feeling or influence living within. He or she has the Holy Spirit indwelling and working within to fulfill the will of God.

These facts emphasize the importance of the true Christian coming to know, understand, appreciate and experience the person, work, and ministry of the Spirit in his or her life. Listed below are a few of His ministry duties:

- The Holy Spirit brings to the heart the revelation of the Father and the Son (see John 14:15-26).
- The Holy Spirit indwells the true Christian's spirit (Romans 8:9; 1 Corinthians 3:16; 6:17; 1 John 2:27).
- The Holy Spirit brings about the new birth (see John 3:3, 5-6).
- The Holy Spirit leads the Christian (Matthew 4:1).
- The Holy Spirit guides the Christian into all truth (John 16:13).
- The Holy Spirit convicts individuals (John 16:8).
- The Holy Spirit directs men and women in the service of Christ (see Acts 8:29; 10:19; 16:6, 7).
- The Holy Spirit imparts spiritual gifts to the members of the body of Christ (see 1 Corinthians 12:7-11).
- The Holy Spirit empowers the Christian to witness (Acts 1:8).
- The Holy Spirit glorifies the Lord Jesus Christ (John 16:14).
- The Holy Spirit will bring about the resurrection and immortality to the true Christians' bodies in the last day (see Romans 8:11; 1 Corinthians 15:47-51; 1 Thessalonians 4:15-18).

The Holy Spirit in the life of the Church

One of the truths of God's Word that seems to be lost to many local churches today is the promise that the Holy Spirit would come after Jesus Christ was glorified after His death, burial, resurrection and ascension (see John 7:38-39). The Holy Spirit did come on the Day of Pentecost. He came as the Executive Agent of the Godhead to build the church that the Lord Jesus said He would build (see Matthew 16:16-20). It is the Spirit's indwelling work that seems to mark the difference between the Old and New Testament saints. Therefore the Holy Spirit's indwelling work is the distinguishing mark of the New Testament Church. In the Old Testament the Spirit descended on special persons, equipping and filling them but not remaining or indwelling continually—*as He does today.* Jesus promised His disciples that the Holy Spirit would come and dwell with them *and in them* and that, as the Comforter, *He would abide with them forever* (John 14:16-17). In his book, The

Foundations of Christian Doctrine, Kevin J. Conner suggests that the major features of the Holy Spirit's work in the church include the following:

- The Holy Spirit formed the church into a corporate structure, the body of Christ on the Day of Pentecost.
- The Holy Spirit baptizes the living members into the body of Christ (see 1 Corinthians 12:13).
- The Holy Spirit formed the church to be the new and living temple of God, setting believers into their places as living stones in the New Covenant temple (see 1 Corinthians 3:16; 6:16; Ephesians 2:20-22).
- The Holy Spirit brings the anointing, illumination and direction to the church as the New Covenant Priestly Body (see II Corinthians 1:21; Psalm 133:1-2; ` John 2:20, 27; Ephesians 1:17-18; Acts 10:38; 1 Corinthians 12:12-13).
- The Holy Spirit brings gifts and graces to the members of the church (see 1 Corinthians 12:4-11, 28-31; Romans 12:6-8; Galatians 5:22-23).[22]

The Lord Jesus is the Head of the Church in heaven and directs His affairs in His Body, the Church, through the Holy Spirit. **It is the Holy Spirit:**

- Who is building us into the image of Christ.
- Who calls, quickens, energizes and equips the various ministries in the Church.
- Who calls, quickens, energizes and equips every member of the Body of Christ according to their specific place (Please study: Acts 13:1-3; 15:28; 20:28; 1 Corinthians 12:8-11; Ephesians 4:8-12; 1 Peter 1:12; 1 Corinthians 2:1-5; Acts 1:8).

After reading this section, I'm sure that you will agree that for hundreds of years the Holy Spirit has been hindered in His work in the church. Many attempt to do their church work and work of the church without Him.

Hopefully the church will come to *know* that because something *has not* been practiced for hundreds of years does not make it wrong. And because something *has been* practiced for hundreds of years does not make it right.

A check of church history reveals that the apostolic Christian church of Pentecost fell silent about A.D. 100, after the death of the apostle John, reappearing about A.D. 150 a totally different church. Under constant persecution many of the Church fathers were martyred; others made some compromises with the state. However, persecution of the Christians intensified as they were given the choice of denouncing Christ and claiming Caesar as lord to live or chose death. Many gladly chose death considering it a privilege to suffer death for the cause of Christ. The church suffered ten persecutions, the first in the year A.D. 67, under Nero through the tenth persecution under Diocletian in A.D. 303.

In Fox's Book of Martyrs, we read, *"Although one apostle had betrayed Him; although another had denied Him, under the solemn sanction of an oath; and although the rest had forsaken Him"* .... *The history of His resurrection gave a new direction to all their hearts, and, after the mission of the* **Holy Spirit imparted new confidence to their minds.** *The powers with which they endued emboldened them to proclaim His name, to the confusion of the Jewish rulers, and the astonishment of Gentile proselytes.*[23]

"He is no fool who gives what he cannot keep—
to gain what he cannot lose"

Jim Elliot, Missionary "1956"

And yet, notwithstanding through all these continual persecutions and horrible punishments, the Church *daily increased, deeply rooted in the doctrine of the apostles and of men apostolical, and watered plenteously with the blood of saints.*[24]

If you are searching for the answer to your church's non-relevancy, the best place to begin is with the New Testament and the Book of Acts because it describes the ministry of the first group of *Spirit-filled believers.* The New Testament church was an exciting and powerful church on their continuing mission to "make disciples" and "extend the kingdom of God."

By today's standards, it may have been crude, undisciplined, to many unbecoming, un-prestigious, poor taste, and irreverent; however, you never notice those things while reading the Book of Acts. What grips you is the *demonstration of power!* At that time in the church God moved in response to prayer. Miracles accompanied the saving power of Jesus Christ. Within the parameters of the church's influence, not only were the lost redeemed, but the lame walked, the blind received their sight and the oppressed were delivered from demonic powers.

It was a community of believers *admittedly imperfect* but spiritually and dynamically alive. Even though the church had been despised by the society around it; no one ever accused it of being boring, dull or dead. Certainly those early Christians were more interested in manifesting orderly worship services. They were more concerned with Christian love than correct liturgy, more concerned with being found faithful than being found popular. *". . . . for with regard to this sect we know that everywhere it is spoken against"* (Acts 28:22).

Comparing the New Testament church with our churches today, undoubtedly one of two things must have taken place:

- Either God deliberately deprived the church of the Pentecostal power, with its supernatural gifts and powers (the rational we hear throughout America)—or the church has somehow lost contact with Pentecost as an essential life-giving continuing experience.
- The second proposal is the true one. The fastest growing churches around the world are Pentecostal. The resurgence

of Pentecostal power on every continent is evidence enough. Church history bears out the fact that the spiritual gifts never completely died out of the church. Though *continuously rejected or just ignored,* they have always been present, flaring up into view during times of renewal of or revival.

The Pentecostal Movement

In 1906, William J. Seymour, a black holiness preacher from Houston, Texas was invited to preach in a black holiness church in Los Angeles pastored by the Reverend Mrs. Julia Hutchins. Seymour preached his first sermon, proclaiming the *"initial evidence"* of the baptism in the Holy Spirit was "speaking in tongues" (as the church had done on the Day of Pentecost). This was offensive and revolutionary teaching, and so He was locked out of the church. Since practically all Christians claimed to be baptized in the Spirit:

- Evangelicals believe it happens at the time of conversion.
- Holiness people believed at the time of their "second blessing" or "entire sanctification."

The teaching of a glossolalia, "tongues" attested Spiritual Baptism became the centerpiece of Pentecostal teaching, with Seymour as the apostle of the movement.[25] Home prayer meetings soon gave way to front porch meetings, which drew hundreds of listeners to hear Seymour and his tongue-speaking followers. Soon the crowds became so large that larger quarters were needed for the fast growing group. A search for a larger facility produced an abandoned building at Azusa Street that had been used prior as an African Methodist Church, a stable, and a warehouse. Seymour began holding services there with the congregation of both blacks and whites.

Revival broke out and lasted for three and a half years at Azusa Street, services were held three times a day—morning, afternoon and night. Tongues-speaking was the central attraction, but healing the sick ran a close second. It soon became apparent that Seymour was the leading personality in the Los Angeles Pentecost.[26]

Nothing was able to stop the momentum of the renewal at Azusa Street; however, "Pilgrims to Azusa" came from all parts of the United States, Canada, and Europe. They in turn spread the fire in other places. Gaston B. Cashwell of the Pentecostal Holiness Church came to Azusa Street blacks asking to be prayed for received the baptism and a few months later after a meeting in Dunn, North Carolina, and a Southern preaching tour led several Holiness denominations into the Pentecostal fold.[27] C.H. Mason, head of the Church of God in Christ of Memphis, Tennessee, came to Azusa in November 1906 and received the Pentecostal experience. H.G. Rodgers and other future pillars he Assemblies of God were baptized under Cashwell's ministry. From Azusa to Canada, Oslo, Norway opened the first Pentecostal work in Europe 1906, to Germany, France, Russia, Italy, Brazil, and Argentina.

Thus, within a short time, the Azusa Street Pentecost became a worldwide move of the Holy Spirit. I believe the Holy Spirit returned [after a 1100 year hindrance], fully to the church worldwide through the Azusa Street revival.

Baptism in the Holy Spirit (Unity)

One of the most destructive forces in the church today is conflict among Christians. Divisions and personality differences among the membership of the church have destroyed lives, families, and brought the gospel of Jesus Christ to non-affect. So, if the church is to fulfill its calling, **Christians must live in unity.** The big thing with many local churches today is numbers. However, most are in disunity. For example, there is no strength in a snow flake, but a thousand snow flakes rolled into a snow ball can be dangerous. If that snow ball was added to a hundred thousand pounds of snowflakes we could have a snow slide capable of wiping out a whole village.

O how effective we would be if we can unite all of our different factions into a single Christian unity. The apostle Paul stresses unity in Ephesians 4:3. He exhorts Christians to be:

> *"Eager to maintain the unity of the Spirit in the bond of peace."*

When we speak of baptisms, normally we think of water baptism or maybe sprinkling. Some even speak of infant baptism. Others say it must be performed only upon adults who understand the meaning of faith and baptism. Paul exhorts, *"for by One Spirit we **were all baptized** into one body; whether Jews or Greeks, whether slaves or free; and have **all** been made to drink into one Spirit"* (I Corinthians 12:13). Emphasis is mine throughout.

The baptism in the Spirit makes even more public our membership in the body. With the Holy Spirit baptism we are **one**—the **ONENESS** of **JESUS' BODY.** That is the **ultimate purpose** of the baptism in the Spirit.

However, the baptism in the Holy Spirit is also a **supernatural seal** that is given to each **individual member** by which Jesus Christ acknowledges him or her as a part of His body, made one with Him in His death and resurrection. John the Baptist said,

> *".... This is the One that baptizes with the Holy Spirit"*
>
> (John 1:33).

There is no one else in Scripture to whom that privilege is given but Jesus Christ. Remember always that the ultimate purpose of the Holy Spirit baptism is unity of Christ's body. The baptism accomplishes this by making [born again] *individual members* of the body effective agents by bringing them to Christ.

The unity of the Spirit baptism will be produced in them by the Spirit. Apart from this unity, any other method of achieving any unity is impossible—many local churches settle for just being united. United is not one and therefore is not unity!

Love and Unity

In John 17, Jesus said that our *love* and *unity* would be a witness to the world. He prayed that Christians *"may all be one . . . . that the world may believe that thou hast sent Me"* (v. 21 KJV). The degree to which division and hostility reign in the church is the degree to which the Holy Spirit will be hindered making the church effective in the community. Our witness is neutralized by our unwillingness to maintain the unity which the Spirit has already produced in us. The world pays no attention to a divided church. It is important that when we true Christians meet together, we realize that we are called to:

- Understand one another.
- Forbear one another.
- Pray for one another.
- Forgive one another.
- Be kind and tender-hearted.
- Not holding grudges.
- Not being bitter.
- Not being resentful.
- Not being hateful toward one another.

Another barrier to church unity is our classifying of Christians by their spiritual gifts or organizations to which they belong. We can't say that only Pentecostals are Christians or those operating in certain spiritual gifts set them above all others. We must realize that the unity of the Spirit will be found in people of many different groups and we must recognize that fact. It is our responsibility to maintain the unity of the Spirit in the bond of peace wherever we find brethren in Christ. Paul says in Romans 14:1:

> *"Receive one who is weak*
> *in the faith,*
> *but not to disputes*
> *over*
> *doubtful things."*

We are not to cast him or her out but to receive them even though he or she does not see as clearly as you do. This is so important today as spiritual ignorance and confusion in world views are on the increase with each succeeding generation. Nevertheless, we are not to pass judgment on them with our reasoning or opinions, but receive them.

We recognize them as brethren if he or she manifests love for Jesus Christ, no matter what label they may be. That is Christ's aim in the baptism of the Holy Spirit. We must realize that our relationships are more important than the temporary issues that divide us.

STUDY GUIDE: CHAPTER 9

RECEIVING THE PROMISE OF THE FATHER

1. The Holy Spirit is not an _____. He is a Person.

2. List (below) several hindrances that result from considering the Holy Spirit and influence or feeling.

3. What is the distinguishing mark of the New Testament church?

4. The Lord Jesus directs His affairs in His body, _____ _____ through the Holy Spirit.

5. Between A.D. 67 and A.D. 305, the church suffered _____ persecutions.

6. The Azusa street revival lasted three and one half years with a black preacher _____ as the leading personality.

7. Through the Azusa street revival, the Holy Spirit sparked a worldwide Pentecostal Movement out of which came The Church of God in Christ, the Assemblies of God Denomination, and several other Pentecostal denominations.

Chapter 10

WHEN POWER COMES TO CHURCH

"But unto every one of us is given grace according to the measure of the gift of Christ. And He Himself gave some to be apostles, some prophets, some evangelists, and some pastors and teachers, for the equipping of the saints, for the work of ministry, for the edifying of the body of Christ, till we all come to the unity of the faith and the knowledge of the Son of God, to a perfect man, for the measure of the stature of the fullness of Christ"
(Ephesians 4:7, 11-13).

Do you know your purpose in life? There are numerous people who struggle through the day-to-day frustrations of life never fulfilling their God-given purpose. These same people invest a lot of time and energy expending *natural gifts* and *abilities,* but what they do fails to have any lasting significance.

In prior chapters I have stressed a proper way for the church to make a difference in the world, the biblical way. God has given each one of us a wonderful opportunity to join with Him in *His* work using *His* gifts. One of the most important things we can do is make a passionate search for significance as we put into *practice* the *Spiritual gifts* God has entrusted to us. The reward of finding and putting into practice your spiritual gift or gifts is the personal blessing of knowing that you are biblically in the will of God (Study Romans 12:1-6).

In the last chapter, we studied that the church is one body, and every member is to strive to keep *oneness* and *unity* of the Spirit.

But believers are not only *unified*, they are also *diversified.* Earlier I used the example of snowflakes each one different than the others, however, when rolled into a snow ball, their differences are molded into one-ness. What are the differences between Christians? The differences are Spiritual gifts. A Spiritual gift is defined as a special attribute given to every member of the body of Christ according to God's grace for use within the context of the body. Each Christian is empowered and energized with supernatural potential to minister communicating the knowledge, power, and love of Jesus Christ. Another important point to remember is the Holy Spirit gives us the grace to use our gifts. Several benefits you receive by having Spiritual gifts:

- You benefit in your personal life making you healthier for serving others.
- The entire church benefits as a new vigor and vitality enters into the church's life.
- They will help you to know God's will for your life.

We prove God's will as we understand our particular gift and its function within the body, and then use that gift accordingly (Look again at Romans 12:1-6). A good steward takes the resources entrusted to him or her and uses them for the purpose [of edifying the body] for which the Master designed them. The results will be:

- Each member will know his or her spiritual job description (see 1 Peter 4:10).
- All members will be able to work together in love, harmony and effectiveness (see 1 Corinthians 14:1a).
- Pride, envy, and false humility will be avoided (see Romans 12:3).
- The whole body will mature (see Ephesians 4:11-14).
- The local church will grow (Ephesians 4:12, 16).
- And God will be glorified (see 1 Peter 4:10-11).

Jesus said, "On this rock **I will build** My Church, and the gates of hell **shall not** prevail against it" (Matthew 16:18a).

God gave Moses the pattern and **all** the details [recorded in some forty chapters of the Bible] for the building of the Tabernacle. He left absolutely nothing to the imagination of humankind. Christ gave the apostles the pattern and **all** the details for His Church in the New Testament [Study the Book of Acts, the Epistles and the Book of Revelation]. Like the Father, He left nothing to the imagination of humankind. Many of the local churches are totally failing or presenting a form of godliness because the leaders are not building [the people] according to pattern! In these churches the Holy Spirit, who is Christ's Chief architect is silenced and never consulted about anything in reference to the building of these so-called Christian churches. Many of them are building *their* own churches on the backs of the people of God, who in reality is [the church]. We often hear, "My church!" or "Those people!" In the Old Testament the priests were **commanded to** dress according to pattern. In the New Testament pattern we are **commanded to** dress according to pattern our vestment is a robe of righteousness. I will never understand why we as God's priests today try to impress the world through natural dress and that can only be accomplished by dressing down and in too many cases laying aside the robe of righteousness. The Old Testament natural example of dress sets the pattern for our New Testament spiritual example of dress. Now that we are clear on who we are [priests] and whose we are [Christ's]; we can move on to what we do [gifts] of service.

Preparation for Service

To many people, churches and even some denominations, spiritual gifts are treated as a medal or trophy that they have won. So wear it proudly and show the congregation who you are! In theology the gifts are classified in various categories, one categorizes some of the gifts as "sign gifts." It appears that some people think these are actually "show gifts." They seem to be trying to intimidate, belittle or outshine the other congregants. Whether the gifts are classified as sign, show, helps or what; they are **all** gifts of service to others. We are to equip and edify the body of Christ for the work of evangelistic ministry. I'm sure that this truth is muddled in many instances as some leaders lead people to believe the service is personally for them. God forbid! Enough of that!

In the Old Testament every detail concerning the Tabernacle was taken care of by priests even down to the care, cleaning and maintaining of the utensils and all other equipment, to include the altars and keeping the holy flame burning for fifteen hundred years. Their service was marked by **"lest ye die."** (KJV)

Ministry in the New Testament church is no exception. God gave this revelation to the apostle Paul which he describes for us as God's way of touching and changing the world. He turns to the provision made by the Holy Spirit for the church to be dynamic and effective as it functions in the world. Our service is marked by **"as unto the Lord."** He writes, *"Grace was given to each of us according to the measure of Christ's gift"* (Ephesians 4:7). In his book "Body Life" Ray Stedman draws out two tremendous points from this brief passage:

- The *gifts of the Holy Spirit* for ministry, which is given to every true Christian without exception.
- The new remarkable *power* by which that gift may be exercised.

Further he points out that there seems little doubt that here is where the early church began with new converts. The new convert was immediately taught that the Holy Spirit of God had not only imparted to him or her the *life* of Jesus Christ, but had also equipped them with a *spiritual gift* or *gifts* which they are then responsible to discover and exercise.[28] The apostle Peter writes, *"As each has received a gift, employ it for one another, as good stewards of God's varied grace"* (1 Peter 4:10). It is vitally important that you discover the gift or gifts you possess.

Varieties of Gifts (Ephesians 4; 1 Corinthians 12; Romans 12; 1 Peter 4)

Again, a Spiritual gift is a specific capacity or function given to each true Christian directly by the Spirit of God. It is important that we understand that these gifts are not hereditary nor do we generate them ourselves; they are imparted to us by the Spirit Himself. The spiritual gift imparted to us by the Holy Spirit denotes our job description in the body of Christ, the church. Please note the gifts listed below are in alphabetical order only:

ADMINISTRATION (1 Corinthians 12:28)

This gift is the special ability that the Spirit gives to certain members of the body of Christ to understand clearly the immediate and long range goals of a particular unit of the body of Christ and to devise and execute plans for the accomplishment of those goals. (Acts 27:11).

APOSTLE (Ephesians 4:11)

This gift is the special ability that God gives to certain members of the body of Christ to assume and exercise general leadership over a number of churches (that they established) with extraordinary authority in spiritual matters which are spontaneously recognized by these churches. For example see 1 Thessalonians 2:6.

CELIBACY (1 Corinthians 7:7-8)

This is the special ability that God gives to certain members of the body of Christ to remain single and enjoy it; to be unmarried and not suffer undue sexual temptations. i.e. Matthew 19:10-12 "for Christ's sake"

DISCERNING OF SPIRITS (1 Corinthians 12:10)

This gift is the special ability that the Spirit gives to certain members of the body of Christ [all mature Christians should have] to know with assurance whether certain behavior purported to be of God is in reality divine, human or satanic. i.e. 1 Thessalonians 5:19-22; 1 Corinthians 6:1-6).

EVANGELISM (Ephesians 4:11)

This gift is the special ability that the Spirit gives to certain members of the body of Christ to share the Gospel with unbelievers in such a way that men and women become Jesus' disciples and responsible members of the body of Christ. i.e. Acts 8:4-6; 21:8; 8:8:26-40 Phillip.

EXHORTATION (Romans 12:6-8)

This gift is the special ability to minister words or comfort, consolation, encouragement, and counsel to other members of the body of Christ in such a way that they feel helped and healed. i.e. 2 Corinthians 1:1-7 God comforts Paul

EXORCISM (Acts 8:1-4)

This gift is the special ability to cast out demons and evil spirits. i.e. Acts 16:16-18 Paul and the slave girl.

FAITH (Ephesians 2:8)

This gift is the special ability to discern with extraordinary confidence the will and purpose of God for the future of His work. [For all Christians] i.e. move mountain Matthew 17:14-21.

GIVING (Romans 12:8)

This gift is the special ability to contribute material resources to the work of the Lord with liberality and cheerfulness. i.e. Philippians 4:16-19.

HEALING (1 Corinthians 12:9, 28, 30)

This gift is the special ability to serve as human intermediaries through whom it pleases God to cure illness and restore health apart from the use of natural means. i.e the leper Matthew 8:1-4.

HELPS (1 Corinthians 12:28)

This gift is the special ability to invest the talents one has in the life and ministry of others of the body, thus enabling the person to increase the effectiveness of his or her spiritual gifts. i.e. Acts 9:36.

HOSPITALITY (1 Peter 4:9-10)

This is a special ability to provide an open house and a warm welcome for those in need of food and lodging. i.e. Hebrews 13:1-2 "strangers"

INTERCESSION (Romans 8:26-27)

This gift is the special ability to pray for extended periods of time on a regular basis ans see frequent and specific answers to their prayers to a degree such greater than the average Christian. i.e. Hannah, 1 Samuel 1:9-18.

INTERPRETATION OF TONGUES (1 Corinthians 12:10)

This gift is the special ability given to certain members of the body of Christ to make known in the vernacular the message of one who speaks in tongues.

KNOWLEDGE (1 Corinthians 12:8)

This gift is a special ability to discover, analyze, and clearly clarify ideas which are pertinent to the growth and well being of the church. i.e. "without pride" 1 Corinthians 8:1-2.

LEADERSHIP (Romans 12:8)

This gift is the special ability to set goals in accordance with God's purpose for the future and to communicate these goals to others in such a way that they voluntarily and harmoniously work together to accomplish those goals for the glory of God. i.e. "family" "church" 1 Timothy 3-5.

MARTYDOM (1 Corinthians 13:1-3, 8)

This gift is the special ability to undergo suffering for the faith even to the point of death while consistently displaying a joyous and victorious attitude which brings glory to God. "death" is ok Acts 20:24.

MERCY (Romans 12:8)

This gift is the special ability to feel genuine empathy and compassion for individuals, both Christian and non-Christian, who suffer distressing physical, mental, or emotional problems and to translate that compassion into fully-done deeds which reflect Christ's love and alleviate suffering. i.e. "debilitating disease" Luke 17:11-14.

MIRACLES (1 Corinthians 12:10, 28)

This gift is the special ability to serve as intermediaries through whom it pleases God to perform powerful acts that are perceived by observers to have altered the ordinary course of nature. i.e. "Tabitha" Acts 9:36-41.

MISSIONARY (1 Corinthians 9:19-23)

This gift is the special ability to minister whatever other spiritual gifts they have in a second culture. i.e. Paul Galatians 2:7-14.

PASTOR (Ephesians 4:11)

This gift is the special ability to assume a personal responsibility for the spiritual welfare of a group of believers. "leads" Hebrews 13:7, 17.

PROPHECY (Ephesians 4:11)

This gift is the special ability to receive and communicate an immediate message of God to His people through a divinely-appointed utterance. i.e. Agabus Acts 21:10, 11.

SERVICE (Romans 12:6, 7)

This gift is the ability to identify the unmet needs involved in a task related to God's work, and to make use of available resources to meet those needs and help accomplish the desired goals. i.e. "others" Luke 22:24-27.

TEACHER (Ephesians 4:11)

This gift is the special ability to communicate information relevant to the health and ministry of the body of Christ and its members in such a way that others will learn. i.e. "not wavering" Ephesians 4:13-14.

TONGUES (1 Corinthians 12:10, 28)

This gift is the special ability to speak to God in a language they have never learned and to receive and communicate an immediate message of God to His people through a divinely anointed utterance in a language they have never learned. "Gentiles" Acts 10:24-28.

VOLUNTARY POVERTY (1 Corinthians 13:1-3)

This gift is the special ability to renounce material comfort and luxury and adopt a personal lifestyle equivalent to those living at the poverty level in a given society in order to serve God more effectively. i.e. "Jesus" Matthew 8:20.

WISDOM (1 Corinthians 12:7, 8)

This gift is the special ability to know the mind of the Holy Spirit in such a way as to receive insight into how given knowledge may best be applied to specific needs arising in the body of Christ. "ask" James 1:5-6.[29]

Remember always that the ultimate purpose of Spiritual gifts is the edification and unity of Christ's body. They accomplish this by making individual members of the body effective change agents, *"Till we all come in the unity of the faith, and of the knowledge of the Son of God unto a perfect man, unto the measure of the stature of the fullness of Christ: that we henceforth be no more children, tossed to and fro, and carried about with every wind of doctrine, by the sleight of men, and cunning craftiness, whereby they lie in wait to receive"* (Ephesians 4:13-14).

STUDY GUIDE: CHAPTER 10

WHEN POWER COMES TO CHURCH

1. The biblical way for a church to make a difference in the world is to join Christ in His work using His gifts.

2. Believers are not only unified but also _____.

3. A Christian's spiritual gift or gifts are his or her _____ _____.

4. In the early church, new converts were taught that the Holy Spirit had not only imparted to him or her the _____ of _____, but also had equipped them with a _____ which they are responsible to discover and _____.

5. The ultimate purpose of spiritual gifts is _____ and _____ of the body.

SECTION 4

GIVE YOURSELF AWAY

Chapter 11

TAKE IT TO THE STREETS

*"For though I am free from all men, I have made myself a servant to all, that I might win the more; and to the Jews I became as a Jew, that I might win Jews; to those who are under the law, as under the law, that I might win those who are under the law; to those who are without law, as without law (not being without law toward God, but under law toward Christ), that I might win those who are without law; to the weak I became as weak, that I might win the weak, **I have become all things to all men, that I might by all means save some.** Now this I do for the gospel's sake, that I may partake of it with you"*

(1 Corinthians 9:19-23).

In the first ten chapters, I attempted to show **who we are in Christ,** in the remaining chapters of the book, I want to emphasize **what we do, in Christ.** I emphasize, in Christ because today much of what is said to be done in Christ is actually done in self. In the passage above, the apostle Paul glorified in a "free gospel of grace!" One writer expressed it, "Paul's pay was to get no pay!" He preached the gospel willingly and rejoiced at the privilege to do so. Two tragedies really hurting the spread of the true gospel of Christ today are those Christians who look upon their responsibilities as burdens instead of blessings; and those who are by their actions and behaviors are the focus instead of the gospel they preach.

"But even if I do not preach willingly, says Paul, "I would still have to preach, because God has committed a stewardship to me." There is a practical [*what we do*] principle here: **we should do absolutely nothing that would reflect negatively on the grace of God and the free offer of salvation.** What are the sinners thinking when they see Christians in the foyers of the local Walmart or other store asking them for donations to support a ministry effort? Yet, they have nothing to say to him or her about the love of Jesus. Another situation that I'm sure has a negative affect on the sinner is the thirty minutes taking the offering, all the while scolding the people for not giving enough.

Some pastors dare not offend members who are "big givers." Others are afraid to challenge the status quo or antiquated tradition.

Win as many as possible

Though the apostle Paul could have enjoyed many liberties:

- He had a right to eat what he wanted to.
- He could have married.
- He could have received a salary.

He willingly gave these rights and privileges up and made himself the servant of all men—that he might **win them to Christ!** All that he did was out of love never of fear! Paul does not say that it is wrong to use these privileges. The Scripture says, "The laborer is worthy of his hire." It is right for Christians to support those who serve them in the Lord. Those who preach the gospel should live from the gospel. God commanded that it be that way. We would do well to study these character qualities of Paul. Notice:

- He put his ministry of the gospel above his personal desires.
- He was willing to conform to the customs of other people, whether Jew or Gentile, in order to bring them to Christ.

For example, see his Nazirite vow (Acts 21:23). Paul did not observe Jewish customs with the Gentiles.
- He willingly made himself the servant.
- He would never compromise his standards.
- He tried to understand those who needed Christ.
- He laid aside his privileges.
- He met them where they were in their experiences.
- He was a Jew, so he used this as a key to open the Jews hearts to the gospel.
- He was a Roman citizen, so he used this as a key to open the door of the gospel to the Gentiles.
- Paul wanted no master but Christ.

He had compassion for the weak and encouraged them—*"All things to all men"* (v. 22). In other words he simply means the wonderful ability of accommodating ourselves to others, understanding them, and seeking to lead them into the knowledge of Christ. Paul used tact to get contact; he willingly sacrificed his own privileges to win the lost.

Take it to the street

I was reading the morning newspaper and two articles jumped out at me. The first titled **[Judge's order halts prayers]** a federal court judge issued a preliminary injunction Wednesday ordering a county board of Commissioners to halt their practice of opening government meetings with prayer. The ACLU accused the board of violating the First Amendment provision ordaining the separation of church and state by routinely praying to Jesus Christ to start its meeting.

The second titled **[Initiative aims to ease gay students' concerns],** here concerned with recommendations about what is needed to help LGBT, (lesbian, gay, bisexual, and transgender students) feel more welcome. They include creating sensitivity training, establishing a student group, more activities for LGBT students and the creation of a LGBT office or center. The objective seems to be "no matter what we have to destroy." The spokesperson stated, "our sentiment on campus is that we are a community that **celebrates diversity** and **demands inclusivity!"** I am not bringing these items up for debate. My concern is, are we educating our people on the big push that's being launched in this country to redefine Christianity by hallowing out the truth of God's Word? For example Christianity is **exclusive not inclusive.** What makes Christianity exclusive? The Founder, Jesus Christ said, "**Unless** one is born again, he [or she] cannot see the kingdom of God" (John 3:3). There are those who teach that there are other ways to God. Jesus said, "I am the way, the truth, and the life. **No one comes to the Father except through Me"** (John 14:6). Emphasis is mine. "Be holy for I am holy" (1 Peter 1:16). Christianity is life in Christ! There seems to be a satanically influenced attitude to destroy this nation—by destroying the foundation upon which it has stood for more than two hundred years. Notice his [take down] strategy, using the subtle weapon of evil, the secularization of:

- The [required] relationship with God and His moral law
- The family and the home
- Education for all
- Government
- Christianity

The Bible says, *"The devil has come down to you, having a great wrath, **because he knows that he has a short time"** (Revelation 12:12b). The devil is angry knowing he has but a short time. He lost the fight at Calvary to Jesus Christ. Now he is waging war against the church, the children of the kingdom before his time is up.

Don't let Satan destroy your foundations

God's Word must remain a lamp unto our feet and a light unto our path; permeating our every thought in every area of life. Christ and His early church are our examples. If we understand that God's moral law is under attack, then we must make a decision to stand for Him. The recent Zimmerman case should be a wake-up call for all true Christians. The sequestered jury had to make a decision based on the legality of the law—totally separated from God's moral law. The Christians were commanded by the Roman [government] to reject Jesus Christ as their Lord and King and render their allegiance to Caesar or face death. Church history reflects that many went over to Caesar's side, but the true church chose death. Earlier I quoted the great theologian Francis Schaffer's statement, "One day we will wake up and find that the America we knew is gone." Our nation's [government] of the people, by the people and for the people is slipping away from us.

The people of California voted for proposition 8 which stated that marriage is defined as the union of one man and one woman, that was the will of seven million people based on **God's moral law**, the people had spoken. The Supreme Court spoke and it was struck down by the **people's legal law**. America is shaking her fist in the face of God! They are shouting we want what we want—and we want it NOW!" God has elected to answer through His true children. If we refuse to act NOW, then we to are subject to the wrath of God right along with the deserving counterfeit church. It's not time to take sides—it's time to take over! Take it to the streets! I have been labeled a radical, a rebel and even shunned by denominational peers for preaching and teaching biblical truth. At one time people were expected to "walk the church and denominatioanl line" which is to say be loyal to your party. It seems that has changed to "walk the secular line." God forbid!

STUDY GUIDE: CHAPTER 11

TAKE IT TO THE STREET

1. The apostle Paul glorified in a "_____
   of _____.

2. What was Paul's approach to witnessing to people.?

3. In a few words define secularization.

4. What is the biblical view of marriage?

5. Define God's moral law.

Chapter 12

HAVE A CONTAGIOUS SPIRIT

In the last section, I suggested that the saints take action, by taking it to the street. I believe in civil disobedience, that is biblically-based, but this situation is spiritual and requires a spiritual counter response. **". . . . by My Spirit said the Lord!"**

Normally when we hear the word contagious, we automatically think of some dreaded disease and the threat of catching it. But in this instance, I want to use it in a positive way. As true children of the kingdom, we receive our commands from our Head, who has left life instructions for us through His Holy Spirit and inspired Word. It would be ludicrous and totally out of Christian character to attempt to act for God without the Spirit and the Word of God. God's counter-response to this world is Christ through His Spirit-filled, *unified* body, the Church. That is, a church full of Christians with a contagious spirit. Lest we forget, the ultimate purpose of the baptism of the Holy Spirit is the *unity of the body* and not *division of the body.* Satan knows that, but it seems not many pastors are grasping that truth.

Secular society is trying its best to scratch Jesus Christ's name from the public square, striving to convince Christians that Christianity is a private religion to be practiced inside the walls of the church building. Many pastors and churches have accepted this unbiblical demotion! You can determine if you are a true child of the kingdom, not only by an obvious faith, but whether or not you have a contagious spirit. Early church Christians immediately were out mingling and mixing with the people. They were in Christ and He was in them, [His Spirit and His Word], so every place they went they lived it to the max. Their lives were [one] set apart for the *cause of Christ.*

Their life displayed their spirit of enthusiasm, their spirit of love, their spirit of unusual devotion energized by the Holy Spirit and the Word. They were fired-up for Jesus! The apostle Paul said that we are living letters—read of all men; therefore, all Christians are influential whether true or false. Someone is reading you! I know Christians and I'm sure you do to, who bear a great influence for Christ. By the same token we both probably know some whose influence is negative. That is bad; because it is actually against or antichrist. When an individual does things for convenience and self-interests, it doesn't show them to be *committed* to *anyone* or *anything* outside of their own selfish pursuits.

Hypocrisy

A hypocrite is one who has little problem with talking the walk, but it is another matter when the time comes walking the talk. They don't practice what they preach. Their contagious spirit is for the church house only.

We often see the sign on church bulletins "Enter to Worship and Leave to serve." Some say, "Scatter to serve." That was undoubtedly true of the early church; while they were together they were preparing to go out and permeate the culture and wider society. They went in and began to talk and to preach, and suddenly their Holy Spirit-filled and empowered spirit began to flow through the lives of others. Those who looked on them with ridicule, criticism and snobbery *soon caught their faith.* The Lord added to the church daily. Because these contagious people were Word-fed and Spirit-led, they accomplished much as evidenced by the reproducing of their contagious spirit in others.

I read this story of a humble pastor's visit in the home of a parishioner whose wife explained that her husband was not at home. He said to the lady, "We certainly have missed you all at church, we wish you would come."

"Oh I'm sorry, but my husband has an awful time with his heart. He has to rest and we spend all day Sunday just resting."

He said to her, "Well, I certainly understand that you would not to do anything that would interfere with your husband's health. We all must be careful at this point; I suppose that he is retired."

"Oh, no, no he has a hundred men under him out at the plant, and he has to work five days a week." This man risks a heart attack five days a week but won't risk thirty minutes to hear a positive witness for Jesus.

Quarantine

Webster's dictionary defines quarantine as a restraint on the movement of persons or goods to prevent the spread of pests or disease. In this case it is salvation that the enemy wants to restrain from movement and spreading. The church today has grown apathetic:

- Because the church won't send them a bill, many fall behind in their tithes and offerings or pledges.
- Because the church won't dismiss them out, Church School and Worship services have to fit into their seasonal recreation schedule.
- Because the church says nothing, many of those that believe in prayer won't come to prayer meeting.
- Because they want all of the overtime they can get, small group mission and Bible study have to take a backseat.
- Because it is not in the program, missionary societies pray and socialize regularly but never really get involved in winning people to Christ.
- Because of complacency, little interest is shown in continuing training toward making mature disciples.

This is non-contagious Christianity and it is filling our churches with empty pews. The world doesn't have to worry about catching this disease, our own complacency gives them an inoculation against it. The early Church was contagious because they had love and enthusiasm for their church work (edification) and their work of the church (evangelism and justice). Apathy will automatically set-in in any church when it begins to compromise the truths of God's Word by siding with the world on issues that go against God's moral laws. The Spirit does not lead or indorse anything that violates God's Word, nor His character. Jesus said, "You are the salt of the earth and the light of the world" (Matthew 5:13). As salt we ought to make the word of God palatable for the unsaved and as light give them understanding of the word of God through our life application.

Again, I mention the miracle of the Jewish people. After thousands of years of dispersal over the world, they still are a distinct people, who love their God and Torah. Jesus said, we are in the world but not of the world. If we really believed that like the Jews we to would live sanctified [separated unto God] lives. What have you done for the Lord today? Are there any new subjects in the kingdom of God, because of your witness and testimony? Are you studying the truths of God's word to show yourself approved unto God? Do you turn each day over to the Lord that you may be led of His Spirit?

I found this story in my notes: A large beautiful tree was cut down in the forest. It was put into the stream with the other trees. On the way to the saw mill this mighty Redwood *drifted away* from the other logs. Finally, after some weeks it drifted into the ocean. A sailor approaching the large log in a small boat yelled, "Danger ahead!" But the captain looked past the front of the boat and said, "Never mind, full speed ahead; it's rotten; it's just *driftwood.*" After observing awhile, the world comes to the conclusion, it's not a Christian," just "driftwood." Would there be enough evidence in your life to find you guilty, if being a Christian became classified as a crime?

STUDY GUIDE: CHAPTER 12

HAVE A CONTAGIOUS SPIRIT

1. Define a contagious spirit.

2. Paul said we are _____ read of all men.

3. The early church carried their _____ into the culture and wider society.

4. The early church was contagious because they had _____ _____ and _____ for their church work.

5. What have you done for the Lord today?

Chapter 13

SEEING TOMORROW TODAY

All over this beautiful land, it is not uncommon to see signs at various establishments reading "No Children—Pets Welcome." I have been invited to preach or participate in Seminars and Conferences in some churches; and though the sign is not posted, the attitudes and actions of the people leave little or no doubt; there is no place for children. All of us have experienced the old proverbial frown if a baby cries or a child get noisy in church. In Matthew 19:13, *"Jesus said,*

> *"Let the little children*
> *come to Me,*
> *and do not forbid them;*
> *for of such*
> *is*
> *the kingdom of heaven."*

The Jewish people placed a high value on family life. It was the custom of children to *ask* their parents to pray for them and bless them, and of disciples to make the same request of rabbis. The one who granted the request would lay his hands on them in blessing. One wrote perhaps the disciples thought that Jesus was too busy to be disturbed. Mark's account of this incident says that Jesus was *"indignant"* because His disciples tried to spare Him the intrusion of the mothers and children, and that Jesus took each child in His arms. Christians must live—not in childishness, but in childlike faith, dependent upon the Holy Spirit and the Word of God for mercy and strength. These verses are the charter of Discipleship training in many churches and families:

- Yet, many shallow folk sometimes think it is not right "to force the mind of children into a mold." If we look at the crime rates, I'm sure we agree that that is exactly what we must do as parents though it is not the popular action in the culture—it is the biblical answer to the problem.
- A wise parent does not allow a child to choose his or her own food, games, TV shows etc.
- Though it may not be acceptable in the culture today, the wisdom of parents is required if truth and compassion are to be honored. The culture loves producing weeds!
- Salvation in the faith cannot be delayed until the child is of age, though unthinking parents often make this assumption.
- A child's mind will be shaped by the street, or by some passer-by, if it is not shaped by godly parents.

So these verses underscore the need of Discipleship training, and require the welcoming of children into the body of Christ, the church. The method of training is also indicated. Notice the mothers:

- Wanted their children to hear the words of Jesus.
- Wanted the story of Jesus' life, death and resurrection, and the teaching of His words; because they are central to Christian nurture.
- Wanted their children to catch the feel of Jesus' presence.
- Wanted the influence of people who truly knew that Jesus is an indispensable need.
- The mothers came hoping Jesus would pray, as discipleship rests upon prayer.

Our world is selfish and growing more secular with each passing day. The church has failed miserably to keep children in center place. In the past most 18-29 year olds had some Christian training and worldview through the home, or Church; and as a result, upon leaving home many left the church for a while, but later returned after marriage or entering their career. Today statistics reflect they are *not* returning to Church! The Christian nurture of young people is treated as a side issue today. We are commanded by the Word of God to, *"Train up a child in the way that he [or she] should go and when he [or she] is old he [or she]* **shall** *not depart from it"* (Proverbs 22:6). Our aim should be to develop in each convert upon salvation a "truthful" biblical worldview. That truth lies in the promise that God made here **[shall not]** not should not, or will not, but a command—shall not!:

- The Command—"Train up a child in the way that he [or she] should go!" (Parental responsibility).
- The promise—When he [or she] is old he [or she] *shall not* depart from it." (God's responsibility).
- We have a tendency to embrace the promise but ignore the command.[30]

It is our biblical responsibility—to insure that our children are properly won to Christ and taught a viable biblical worldview. This subject is covered in depth in my book: *"Give Me Jesus;"* which is available from Amazon on line or wherever books are sold. I believe this is the ultimate parental responsibility. The school systems are indoctrinating our children on subjects and issues; which they will definitely be able to handle in life and without frustration **only** if they were properly nurtured on the milk of God's Word.

There is an old saying, "The hand that rocks the cradle rules the world." In other words the person who nurtures your child has the power to put either a Bible or a 9mm pistol in the child's hand. Which will you give that child? Will you give the child a heart for God, or the heart of a thief or murderer? Even in a day when care for children outside the home is a norm, because of employment and other reasons, parental responsibility does not stop there. Parents must check, check, check! If we don't prayerfully train, support and stay involved with our children—the street, secular media and culture will!

Something to ponder: The Holy Spirit was in John the Baptist in his mother's womb at six months (see Luke 1:41). Daniel had God's favor on his life as a teenager (see Daniel 1:9).

Yes! Jesus still loves me

After retiring from the U. S. Army at Fort Bragg and settling in Fayetteville, North Carolina, occasionally on the streets, on the post, or in area churches someone will approach me and inform me that they served under me in one of the units or commands in which I served or churches that I have served as pastor. Many times I have never met them personally as they honorably and successfully served unnoticed. Then there are a few names and people that I will never forget, because they were disruptive, discipline problems, unsuccessful counselees, or intolerable people.

My purpose in sharing that is, if you remember there are some folks like that in your community, work place, church, or school. That group does not include many people when considering the total population. However, a lot of time is spent with them. A few bad apples does not mean the whole harvest is corrupted; an assumption that if not careful cause us to ignores all of the remaining good ones. Somehow those rotten apples can prejudice us against the whole group; and that seems to be the case because of a few rotten apples or troubled people in the news media or neighborhood, everyone in that generation or age group is being cast aside and considered corrupted or corruptible.

Many parents, teachers, pastors, and significant others seem to be washing their hands of this generation of young people. That is so sad because most of them are normal and possess the same aspirations of young people in past generations. Therefore, while we have the reins, perhaps we need renewal and our antiquated programs and methodologies of communicating with them should be updated; [every profession studies to remain current; however so many in Church leadership see no need for it]. Certainly it will help eliminate the growing generational age gap. This "I don't need to know" attitude is further negatively affecting the general society and the Church culture alike.

In spite of what the media and polls reports, the majority of this generation in question, are those ages 18-29 are alive but not so well. While those who are criminally news worthy get the attention, the majority continue to attend community functions, volunteer, become ministers, entrepreneurs, educators and pursue other professions in their own right. Churches continue to provide Church school, annual Vacation Bible Schools, summer camps and mission trips. Additionally, attendance in Bible colleges and schools is up. Numerous Churches are establishing their own discipleship curriculums, and activities to bring their members to maturity in the Lord. The *truth* of God's Word continues to be taught in caring communities. All is not lost as some media and antichrist factions would have you to believe. Christ is still the Head of the Body, the church. He is still on His throne. He has not lost control of the world's governments nor population. No matter what it may look like naturally, the true Church of God is alive and well. It is the secular or counterfeit [newsworthy] church, where the mission has been lost that the body is really suffering. Any church that no longer recognizes Matthew 28:18-19 as the primary mission; and who no longer promotes a biblical worldview undoubtedly has established there own separate agenda for existing. So many churches pursue their own agenda and it is apparent by the empty and lack of young people, especially the 18-29's. Thank the Lord more and more churches are turning back to the Biblical doctrine instead of traditional Church and denominational doctrines [i.e. One Hundred reasons why I am a Baptist, Methodist or what] now some are promoting a biblical worldview; and moving away from secularly created on-line programs. Magdalene and I founded the Bread of Life Bible Institute, with a non-traditional biblical curriculum fifteen years ago. Our mission is to equip the students with a biblical worldview, bringing them to maturity in the Lord and preparing them for meaningful ministry and service. Our purpose is to help bi-vocational pastors and other Church-workers in the smaller churches. Over the years the school has expanded to seven additional campuses in five states. Our model of ministry is not new, just biblical. Several denominational leaders have endorsed our efforts. Our students are referrals through Spirit-filled alumni and present student body recruitments. I think that many churches are looking at the generation through secular eyes and not mission-mindedly. We are non-traditional and non-accredited by choice, allowing us to tailor our curriculum to the needs of the people [spiritually and economically].

This generation demands more than the faith and failures of science and reason upon which many in the prior generation relied! They view the older generation as somewhat suspect. The world has been in turmoil their entire life. The disciplines that the older generation sought as the answer to the nation's social woes enabled us to go to the moon but our moral, social and economic problems were still in place upon our return to the landing pad. They are seeking the spiritual experience that only Christ can provide; however, fewer churches are teaching and preaching the necessity of the salvation experience, spiritually growing into maturity and living a holy life. Additionally, this older generation is not making room for the incoming generation. So they leave! Older Spirit-filled saints should come out of retirement in the churches to mentor them. A "renewed mind" in all generations living present truth could close the generational communication gap in the Church (Study Romans 12:1-8); now prayerfully apply it to your life. Turning back to the Bible and the biblical worldview of the early Church may not change the world, but it will change the Church that will in turn change the world through the power of the Holy Spirit; which is Christ's pattern for His Church.

America's Mission Field

In his book, Winning Children to Christ, George B. Eager wrote, the world's most fruitful mission field is not a particular place. It is not a particular country; as Christian television might lead you to believe. It is certain kind of people—*our* children! No group of people is more susceptible to the gospel as children, and they are everywhere. Why should the fact that children can be saved be surprising to us? To "become as little children" is a primary condition for entering the kingdom of heaven. Jesus said, *"Except you be converted, and become as little children, you **shall not** enter the kingdom of heaven"* (Matthew 18:3).

Eager continues, faith comes easily to children. Their hearts are tender and naturally open. They are honest and sincere. They are deeply moved, when their sins are pointed out to them. We often hear a parent say, "I want my child to wait and receive Christ when he is old enough to know what he is doing." Children should know what they are doing when they come to Christ. But if children are old enough to know when they have sinned, they are old enough to know they need a Savior. The story is told of a little five year old to respond to his mother's question, "Johnny have you been in the jelly?" No momma! Johnny tell me the truth, did you go into the jelly? No momma? Then how did all that jelly get on the front of your shirt? That's why we all need a Savior, like little Johnny, "We have all sinned and come short of the glory of God" (see Romans 3:23).

The never-ending task

Jesus wants all children to come to Him, but before they can come to Him, they must **hear** about Him. It is our job to tell them! Sometime ago I put this little illustration in my files: We think most everybody knows about coke; yet the Coca Cola Company spends millions each year advertising them. With cokes everywhere you go, why do they need to do this? A Coca Cola advertising executive explained why:

- Each year several million people die. They are no longer Coca Cola customers.

- Each year millions of children are born. They have never heard about Coca Cola.
- We have the never-ending job of telling these people about our product.

We Christians have the most wonderful "product" in the world, the people must hear about it:

- Each year millions of children are born into this world. They know nothing about Jesus Christ and His salvation.
- Christians have the never-ending job of telling children everywhere that God loves them and that Jesus died for them that they might belong to Him eternally.

Who can win the children?

Any believer who loves the Lord and loves souls can win children to Christ. To be effective, Christians should:

- **Love children** and believe that they are important.
- Realize that **every child has infinite possibilities** and treat each one as a Very Important Person.
- See that, **without Christ, the child is lost** and "dead in trespasses and sins;" see that every unsaved child needs to be "born again" through faith in Jesus Christ.
- Believe that **children can be saved;** believe that they can understand the essentials of the gospel.[31]
- **Learn to speak to children** on their level of understanding and seek ways of making the gospel plain to them.
- **Learn new ways** of catching and building children's attention when presenting the gospel, making the message entertaining as well as enlightening. No one should bore children with a dull and uninteresting message.
- **Expect results.** A young preacher was discouraged and he went to an older pastor for counsel. The pastor asked, "Do you expect someone to be saved every time you preach?"

"No," I don't expect that!" the young preacher replied."
"Then perhaps that is why you are not winning souls, "said
the pastor."

- **Be filled with the "joy of the Lord."** Children are attracted
  to those persons whose hearts over flow wit contagious joy.
  If they see we have something so good that we can't keep it
  to ourselves, they will want it.

STUDY GUIDE: CHAPTER 13

SEEING TOMORROW TODAY

1. If not shaped by godly parents a child's mind will be shaped by the _____ or by some _____ _____ ?

2. What is the return rate today among the 18-29 years old who leave the Church after leaving home? Explain below:

3. God gave a _____ and then He made a _____ Proverbs 22:6.

4. America's greatest mission field is _____ _____.

5. An effective soul-winner for children should _____, _____, and _____.

Chapter 14

CONTEND FOR THE FAITH

*"Beloved, while I was very diligent to write to you concerning our common salvation, I found it necessary to write to you exhorting you to contend earnestly for the faith which was once delivered to the saints. For certain men have crept in unnoticed, who long ago were marked out for this condemnation, ungodly men, who **turn the grace of our God** into lewdness and deny the only Lord God and our Lord Jesus Christ"*

(Jude 3-4).

Traditionally, in the institutional church anything new or different seems to be automatically suspect and to many of them [nothing should ever be done for the first time]. They have a tendency to see through the rearview mirror rather than out through the front windshield, it is safer that way. Earlier in chapter I spoke of the Reformation church (Sardis) that thrived on the past.

Today while most eyes are glued on what the media thinks is important, there is a fresh move of the Spirit of God and those of us who are caught up in the leadership roles are suffering loneliness and persecution the world over. This move of the Spirit which I reported in an earlier chapter began in 1906 at Azusa Street in Los Angeles. The Spirit did a new thing by using a black preacher named William J. Seymour to spearhead the now world wide Pentecostal Movement. We hear people "speaking in tongues" today across denominational lines and think of it as normal. Seymour and those who pioneered the movement with him were called fanatics, troublemakers and then when you add the fact that though he was black man; many white people where attracted to the services (a minimum of three services a day)—to the point that the revival lasted three and a half years. Gracious that in itself was miraculous!

To this day many people are still hesitant in receiving present truth as reflected in their spiritual life over the fact of God using Seymour [a black preacher] and tongues; which is still too new for the institutional church and they are suffering for that mindset today. There remains a place more segregated than the eleven o'clock hour on Sunday—the church's cemetery. Many Pentecostal and Charismatic Christians around the world celebrated the centennial in 2006 of the Pentecostal Movement; however with few exceptions it did not receive a favorable mention here in America. It is so sad that here many years later in many articles and publications written concerning the Azusa Street revival Seymour is not mentioned at all or his role is minimized.

In 1970, I accepted my calling to teach the *truth* of God's Word. Immediately, I ran into opposition from some pastors who declared that pastor-teacher was one ministry and a person not called to preach could not indulge in it! However, from 1970—my calling into the preaching of the gospel in 1980; God gave me a decade of favor as a teacher and conference speaker across denominational lines and multicultural settings of which my wife and I have so many fond memories, thank you Father for those experiences.

Our next assignment was twenty eight years of pastoral/ teaching ministry in traditional churches. [Between Maryland Bible Institute, Lee Bible College, Heritage Bible College and Liberty University], I received my theological training. Like the man out of which Jesus cast the legion, of unclean spirit, I loved the salvation experiences, deliverance experiences, spiritual gifts, and ministry of the Holy Spirit in the true Pentecostal/ Charismatic settings. Jesus told him to, *"Go home to your friends, and tell them what great things the Lord has done for you, and how He has had compassion on you"* (Mark 5:19). Jesus was referring to Himself as God who *controlled* both the *natural* and the *supernatural* worlds.

He told me to go home and tell them what great things the Lord has done for me. I remember the joyful gleam in many of the old Baptist deacons and saints born in the late 1800's almost home, as the Holy Spirit guided this preacher/ teacher to them, I thought to help them clarify some things, many sat there like hungry children [looking at this new thing that God had put back in the church] but it didn't take me long to find out who was doing the clarifying. That was in the 70's and early 80's; and it was not long before they were gone. My own father [born in the year of the Azusa Street Revival, 1906] use to caution me, "Don't forget the spiritual, son. Don't forget the spiritual."

Magdalene and I have traveled preached and taught quite widely on three different continents and everywhere we go, I find the ministry of the Holy Spirit from the baptism of the Holy Spirit, to the Spiritual gifts, to deliverance and healing are still the topics of interest, discussions, and perhaps controversy among Christians around the world. The sad part of this experience is that many Protestant congregations who have never been taught the Holy Spirit's true purpose and work in the Body of Christ, the Church nor have they experienced the fullness of the Spirit to include their daily walk. Many also shy away from the Book of Acts and the early Church model. As I stated earlier, across denominational lines we hear different interpretations of 1 Corinthians 12:13).

"For by one Spirit
we were
all baptized
into
one body:
whether Jew or Greek,
whether slaves or free;
and
have all
been made to
drink into
one Spirit."

Always remember, "the ultimate purpose of the Holy Spirit baptism is the unity of Christ's body." Additionally, we should remember that there is only one condition required to make a person a child of God and that is saving faith in Jesus Christ (see Galatians 3:26). We need to get back to the truth of God's Word and away from teaching many of the confusing interpretations which equate to false doctrine.

Unity of the Faith

In the last section, we concentrated on the unity of the Body of Christ, the church. In this section we will concentrate on another aspect of unity. Like the prior unity, here the concern is oneness. In Ephesians 4:13, notice:

> *Till we all come into the **unity***
> *of the faith.*
> *and of the knowledge*
> *of the Son of God,*
> *unto a perfect man,*
> *unto the measure of the stature*
> *of the fullness of Christ:*

In Ephesians 4:11, Christ gave five gifts: apostles, prophets, evangelists, pastors and teachers to equip the saints for the work of ministry. All five gifts involve *speech* or *proclamation.* They are very specialized gifts given by Christ Himself to carry out what He began to do and to teach (see Acts 1:1).

These five gifts looked upon as the professional gifts of the church—are given to every Christian *not* in full measure:

- Every Christian should be *as* and apostle in that he or she is serving Christ in a very special ministry and faithfully using the Spiritual gift given to them.
- Every Christian should be *as* prophet in that he or she is claiming God's Word every day.

- Every Christian should be *as* an evangelist in that he or she is bearing witness to the lost.
- Every Christian should be *as* a pastor in that he or she is shepherding and caring for people all time.
- Every Christian should be *as* a teacher in that he or she is teaching the truths of God's Word to all whom he or she knows.

Much of the body of Christ is in jeopardy today because rather than equipping the saints for ministry; the church thinks they are hiring the professional to do the work of ministry. This was a great hindrance and subject of much of my teaching as a pastor in the traditional church. Needless to say it brought on some needless confusion, but I stayed the course. I saw my *primary task* as an equipper, who made disciples and prepared them for the ministry of the church. The church is not the church of God if the members are not doing the work of the ministry. Where the ministry task is left to the pastor it never gets done, for the task a too great.

All believers within a church must be involved in the work of the church ministry. The membership must be equipped to reach the lost and to minister to the needs of a world spiraling downward under the weight of secular evil. Another hindrance to unity is those who are in the church thinking they have it all together; no one comes into the kingdom in that state. If Christians are to be equipped, they must realize that:

- All are broken people.
- No one knows it all.
- In order to be equipped requires that each person must have a teachable spirit.
- Each Christian needs a mentor to hold them accountable.

Contend for the Faith

The ultimate goal here is to bring all into the unity of the faith. We should all believe and speak the same thing biblical doctrine.

The ministers are given to us to keep us from being tossed to and fro, and carried about by every wind of [false] doctrine or false teaching. Jude 3-4 warns and exhorts and it [bears repeating] that we all:

> *"Contend earnestly for the faith which was once for all delivered to the saints. For certain men have* **crept in unnoticed,** *who long ago were marked out for this condemnation, ungodly men, who* **turn** *the grace of God into lewdness and deny the only Lord God and our :Lord Jesus Christ."*

These were false teachers infiltrating the church two-thousand years ago. They were pretending to be the true, who on the surface looked like the real thing, but their intentions from the very beginning were to lead God's people astray. These apostates were Satan's counterfeits most likely as itinerant teachers. They were slick which made them double dangerous. The Scripture characterized by three features:

- They were ungodly.
- They perverted grace.
- They denied Christ.

The apostle Peter weighs in and warns, speaking of these false teachers, *"These are wells without water, clouds carried by a tempest, for whom is reserved the blackness of darkness forever"* (2 Peter 2:17).

- A well without water would be a major disappointment in a hot and dry land. *Likewise, false teachers have a pretense of spiritual water to quench the thirsty souls; actually they produced nothing.*
- The coming clouds would seem to promise rain, but the storm moved around leaving the land dry. *Likewise the false*

teachers might seem to promise spiritual refreshment, but were all show with no substance.

The great blackness of hell awaits them (see Matthew 8:12; Jude 13).

Negligence in doing the Lord's Work

A few years ago someone said, "If you took the traditional [i.e. Baptist, Methodist or Presbyterian] Church's doctrine and put it together with the Holiness/ Pentecostal/ Charismatic experience—you would have a true Christian. I don't know why so many Christians get the impression that spiritual things are just a matter of emotions. However, as a result of this thinking much of what is called spiritual today in some of the churches is void of intelligence and at the same time void of the Spirit. It would be better to just classify much of it as "feel good" religion. Folks that is error! The *call* and *preparation for ministry and practical service* are still required (see Ephesians 4:12). Major incidents through the years have impacted the church theologically; and through carelessness true biblical doctrine is being misconstrued. Each incident in society has in its own its own way affected changes in the church culture:

- In 1963—prayer was taken out of the schools.
- In 1973—abortions became legal. Since then 55 million recorded abortions have been performed.
- In 2013—the approval of same sex marriages.
- Recent court cases reveal a more pronounced move away from moral laws to the embracing of the legal law (may the best trickster win).
- National security is being set at the approval of the secular media, who is telling the government they have no right to keep public opinion out of the loop.
- The media has a compilation of words that they won't use on the air for instance, when was the last time you heard the word "illegitimate" in the media?

- I'm sure that some organizations are poised to pounce on the church with a list of terms or first amendment charges; or claiming something illegal because to them it may seem politically incorrect.

We are often impatient with God for not responding to our requests. But the Scripture says, *"The Lord is not slack concerning His promise, as some count slackness, but is longsuffering toward us, not willing that any should perish but that all should come to repentance"* (2 Peter 3:9). Our troubles are usually of our own making, because we love to follow our own agendas and not follow God's.

- God's agenda does not require periodic updating to be relevant, it does not change.
- For relevancy the society and culture had better line up with the Word of God.
- Agreeing with any of the incidents above is compromise; its time to make a stand on God's moral law which does not change with the secular media and society.
- We walk by faith, not by sight.

We are to be His disciples and like the angels, *"that excel in strength, that do His commandments, hearkening unto the voice of His Word"* (Psalm 103:20). We must be ready to *"Preach the word; be instant in season, out of season; reprove, rebuke, exhort with all longsuffering and doctrine. For the time will come when they will not endure sound doctrine"* (2 Timothy 4:2-3).

And that, knowing the time, that now it is high time to awake out of sleep; for now is our salvation newer than when we believed. The night is for spent; the day is at hand
(Romans 13:11-12).

But sanctify the Lord God in your hearts: and be ready always to give

an answer to every man
that asks you the reason for the hope
that is in you

(1 Peter 3:15).

The apostles Paul and Peter are saying to the Body of Christ today; it is time [*for* us] to wake up, stand up and be prepared to defend God's Word against secularism:

- All Christians should acknowledge the **holiness of Christ** by boldly lifting Him up as the Lord of the universe who is in control of all things.
- I think all true Christians realize that its just a matter of time before through false accusations some of us are going to have to defend our faith. He therefore encourages Christians to have rational answers to respond to those false accusations.
- Each Christian must understand what he or she believes and why they are a Christian, and humbly and biblically express the hope that is in you.

Seeing Tomorrow Today

If we are going to follow God's agenda then we must consider our secret weapon, the Holy Spirit. We are filled with the Spirit *". . . . So that the righteous and just requirement of the law might be fully met in us who live and move not in the ways of the flesh but in the ways of the Spirit [our lives governed not by the standards and according to the dictates of the flesh, but controlled by the Spirit].*

For those who are according to the flesh and are controlled by its unholy desires set their minds on and pursue those things which gratify the flesh, but those who are according to the Spirit and are controlled by the desires of the Spirit set their minds on and seek those things which gratify the Holy Spirit (Romans 8:4-5 Amplified Bible).

The Scriptures distinctly state that the only way to overcome these fleshly desires is to live in the **power** of the Holy Spirit as He works through our spirit to form us into Christlikeness (see Galatians 5:25). Walking each moment by faith in the truths of God's Word under the control of the Holy Spirit; you shall not fulfill the lusts of the flesh (see Galatians 5:16). God has provided a way out; so don't be deceived; compromise nor hypocrisy is an excuse (see Galatians 6:7-8). Walking in the Spirit (reflecting the character of God) characterizes who I am in Christ. The apostle Paul lists this nine-fold fruit produced in us by the Spirit:

- Love—esteem, devotion, mutuality (v.22; 1 Corinthians 13; Romans 8:28).
- Joy—rejoice even among the worse circumstances (v.22; Philippians 4:11).
- Peace—keeps your heart and mind, no anxiety (v.22; Philippians 4:7).
- Longsuffering—power under control (v.22; II Corinthians 6:3-10).
- Kindness—goodness, patience (v.22; 1 Corinthians 13:4).
- Goodness—righteousness (v.22; Romans 15:14; II Thessalonians 1:11).
- Faithfulness—Faithful; faith (v.22: 3:10).
- Gentleness—meekness, submissive, teachable (v.23: II Corinthians 10:1).
- Self-control—temperance, self mastery (v.23; I Corinthians 7:9; 10:23, 31).

Since every true Christian is indwelt by the Holy Spirit—every Christian will manifest the fruit He produces in his or her life. Through these godly character qualities the Christian glorifies God in the world.

Total dependence on the Holy Spirit

The whole life of Jesus as the perfect Man and our Example was governed here on earth by the Holy Spirit. [How much more should the Christians constantly depend upon the Spirit, who is not just upon them but in them]. All that God has for us and desires to do in us will only happen by the operation of the Holy Spirit in our lives and in the church. Therefore, it behooves Christians individually and corporately [the church] to seek the fullness of the Spirit working in their lives (see Ephesians 5:18).

Neither intellectualism, individualism nor any of the many popular "isms" bombarding our society and some local churches today are biblical. We know that well from the Spiritless results apparent in many of our institutional and traditional Churches, whose agenda is normally guided by their past (history).

The Holy Spirit formed the Church on the Day of Pentecost into a corporate structure, the Body of Christ. He baptized the living members into this spiritual body. Therefore, the Day of Pentecost is called the birthday of the church (see Acts 2:1-4; 1 Corinthians 12:12-27; Romans 12:3-8; Ephesians 1:22-23; 4:11). The church here does not refer to any one local assembly but to all true believers everywhere. Are you and your local church led by the Holy Spirit? Are you dependent on Him for all matters of life?

In His book *The foundations of Christian Doctrine,* Kevin J. Conner lists 21 features of the Spirit's work in the life of believers that open their hearts to the fullness of the Holy Spirit:

The work of the Holy Spirit in the Believer

1. The new birth is brought about by the Spirit (John 3:5-6).
2. The Spirit indwells the believer's spirit (Romans 8:9; 1 Corinthians 3:16; 6:17; 1 John 2:27).
3. The Spirit gives assurance of salvation (Romans 8:16).
4. The Spirit fills the believer with Himself (Acts 2:4; Ephesians 5:18).

5. The Spirit baptizes all believers into one body, the Church (1 Corinthians 12:13).
6. The spirit speaks to the believer (Acts 8:29; 1 Timothy 4:1; Revelation 2:7, 11, 17, 29).
7. The Spirit opens the believer's understanding to the things of God (1 Corinthians 2:12).
8. The Spirit teaches the believer, and guides him or her into all truth (John 16:13; 1 John 2:27).
9. The Spirit imparts life (John 6:63; II Corinthians 3:6).
10. The Spirit brings about renewal (Titus 3:5).
11. The spirit strengthens the believer's inner being (Ephesians 3:16).
12. The spirit enables the believer to pray (Jude 20; Romans 8:26-28).
13. The believer to worship in spirit and in truth (John 4:23-24; Philippians 3:3; 1 Corinthians 14:15).
14. The Spirit leads the believer (Romans 8:14).
15. The Spirit enables the believer to put fleshly deeds to death (Romans 8:13).
16. The spirit produces Christ-likeness in character and fruit in the believer's life (Galatians 5:22-23).
17. The Spirit gives a calling to the believer for special service (Acts 13:2-4).
18. The Spirit guides believers into their ministry (Acts 8:29; 16:6, 7).
19. The Spirit empowers the believer to witness (Acts 1:8).
20. The Spirit imparts spiritual gifts to the believers as He wills (I Corinthians 12:7-11).
21. The Spirit will bring about the resurrection and immortality to the believers' bodies in the last day (Romans 8:11; 1 Corinthians 15:47-51; 1 Thessalonians 4:15-18).[32]

The Work of the Holy Spirit in the Church

Not only is the work of the Spirit seen in the individual believer but also seen in the church:

1. The Holy Spirit formed the body of Christ, the church (Acts 2:1-4).
2. The Holy Spirit formed the church to be the new and living temple of God setting believers into their places as living stones in the New Covenant temple (I Corinthians 3:16; 6:16; Ephesians 2:20-23).
3. The Holy Spirit brings anointing, illumination and direction to the church as the New Covenant Priestly Body (II Corinthians 1:21; Psalm 133:1-2; 1 John 2:20, 27; Ephesians 1:17-18; Acts 10:38; 1 Corinthians 12:12-13).
4. The Holy Spirit brings gifts and graces to the members of the church (I Corinthians 12:4-11, 28-31; Romans 12:6-8; Galatians 5:22-23).
5. The Holy Spirit is the Agent of direction and government in the Church. The Lord Jesus is the Head of the Church in heaven and He directs His affairs in His Body by means of the Holy Spirit. It is the Spirit who calls, quickens, energizes, and equips the various ministries of the Church and every member of the Body of Christ according to their particular place (Acts 13:1-3; 15:28; 20:28; 1 Corinthians 12:8-11; Ephesians 4:8-12; 1 Peter 1:12; 1 Corinthians 2:1-5; Acts 1:8).

Thus as Jesus Christ, the Head of the Body was under total control and dominion of the Spirit, and the Spirit was able to flow freely in perfect and unhindered operation, so this must be manifested in the Church today as the visible Body of Christ.[33]

One writer wrote, the Church is to be in the world as a ship is in the ocean—when the ocean gets into the ship it begins to go down. Likewise, when the world gets into the Church and goes unchecked the Church begins to go down. Many summaries of the basic lifestyle of Christians today is essentially no different from the world, if that is the consensus why should it surprise us if our impact on this culture is so limited?

Let's get it right

Our calling is to live out the reality of who we are and whose we are with dignity, kindness, and conviction. We are to model the character of Christ (Galatians 5:22-23) in a world that is skeptical, a world that thinks God doesn't matter. It is time to gear up and take over, no not with guns or 2x4's and the like, but in the example of Christ and the apostles. When Paul spoke to the churches, he was led by *"the meekness and gentleness of Christ"*(2 Corinthians 10:1). Although he used strong language in very serious situations, he more often implored the believers to hear him and encouraged others to adopt this same loving attitude. *"If someone is caught in a sin, you who are **spiritual** should restore him [or her] gently"* (Galatians 6:1 NIV), he said, and advocated the same spirit of gentleness towards those who opposed "sound teaching" (2 Timothy 2:24-25).

Paul did not order the Corinthians to, "Do this!" or "Do that!" Rather he appealed to their wisdom: "I speak to sensible people; judge for yourselves what I say" (1 Corinthians 10:15 NIV). He did not bully them (1 Corinthians 9:22).

Spiritual Authority

Spiritual authority only operates properly where people have happily yielded themselves to it. *It cannot be forced upon the unwilling!* Hearts must be won and trust must be gained. A person who often contends for their own authority is actually betraying the fact that he or she is insecure in their role.

Confrontation is another important responsibility for all church leaders; since it guards the flock of God against error. However, if correction outnumbers encouragement, people have problems receiving it. Unlike the world, God wants His shepherds to treat the flock as friends. When people know they are loved, they will often receive words of rebuke that will hurt, because they believe that "faithful are the wounds of a friend" (Proverbs 27:6). All corrections must be done with love!

To Edify

The ultimate purpose of spiritual authority is to edify or build up the body of Christ. It should be an outworking of the love and devotion the leadership shows to the people. Several ungodly behaviors come to mind that does not edify or build up, but tear down:

- Leaders who dominate.
- Leaders who command and not counsel.
- Leaders with a possessive attitude.
- Leaders who stifle creative thinking.
- Leaders who feel threatened or fear the people.
- Leaders who force their will.
- Leaders who dominate others.
- Leaders who force people to recognize their spiritual authority.

Leaders lead by example. Paul did not say to Timothy, "Let no man despise your youth"—"show them who is in charge!" No, No, he exhorted him to set an example to the believers:

- "in life,"
- "in love,"
- "in faith"
- "in holiness"

From Death to Life

This seems to be the simple Scriptural pattern for passing from death to life, for passing out of the old man and the law, and into newness of supernatural life in Christ and the Holy Sprit. We must yield to the Holy Spirit and a life of righteousness. God's way of righteousness and holiness is not **struggling** but **yielding.** In the process you must come to an end of your efforts and ask the Holy Spirit to take over. "I can't handle this situation, but you can." That doesn't mean you don't need willpower. It means you have to use your willpower differently; you have to use it **not** *to* **try** *to do it yourself.*

Our natural independence causes us to automatically think up a solution any time a problem arises. It takes time to get past that. The sooner the better for it is a life of yielding to the Holy Spirit within us.

STUDY GUIDE: CHAPTER 14

CONTEND FOR THE FAITH

1. Jude admonishes believers to _____ for the _____ once delivered to the saints.

2. William J. Seymour was a black preacher who was credited with pioneering the _____ Movement which became worldwide.

3. The Azusa St. revival lasted for a period of _____ and ½ years.

4. In Eph. 4:11, Christ gave five ministers to the body of Christ. Please list them below:

   _____.

5. The ultimate goal of the Baptism of the _____ _____ is _____.

6. Following the Example, every Christian must _____ totally on the _____.

7. Several incidents in society greatly affected the Church culture and the moral foundations of America. Fill in the blanks.

   - 1963 _____
   - 1973 _____
   - 2013 _____

SECTION 5

TO GOD BE THE GLORY

Chapter 15

STRENGTHENING THE RIGHT HAND OF GOD

"And that He may send Jesus Christ, who was preached to you before, whom heaven must receive until the times of restoration of all things, which God has spoken by the mouths of His Holy prophets since the world began"

(Acts 3:20-21).

The Book of Acts provides the history of the first-century church. All the truths, ministries, doctrines, and supernatural manifestations that were in the early Church *were to continue throughout the Church age.* The law and the tabernacle provided God's *covenant* for proper relationship with Him from the time Moses received the law of God on Mount Sinai until the time of Jesus on the cross.

By His death, burial, and resurrection Jesus fulfilled the law and the *Old Covenant.* He also ushered in a *New Covenant,* which is identified as the *New Testament* in the Holy Bible. In *The Day of the Saints,* Dr. Bill Hamon identifies four major phases of the Church Age. Within each of these ages are shorter periods of time referred to as times, seasons, years, and last days, as well as times of *revival* or *renewal* and *restoration movements.*[34] The Church Age includes all of the following:

- The early days of the Church.
- The great falling away during the Dark Ages.

- The times of *restoration* movements
- The last days or end times until the resurrection and translation of the Saints at Christ's second coming.[35]

Dr. Hamon identifies these four phases by four words: *origination, deterioration, restoration, and destination.*

- The **origination** covers the time of birth of the Church on the Day of Pentecost I A.D. 30, established fully as a separate entity from Judaism in A.D. 70 with the fall of Jerusalem, and expanded the gospel to the ends of the earth by the third and fourth centuries.[36]
- The **deterioration** of the Church covers the period of the great falling away into an apostate condition from the fourth century to the fifteenth century A.D.[37]
- The **restoration** of the Church officially began with the Protestant Movement and has progressed through 500 years of *restoration moves of God.*[38]
- The **destination** of the Church covers the *future and final ministry* of the moral Church and then its resurrection/translation into its immortal reign with Christ during the endless ages to come: *"To Him be glory **in the Church** by Christ Jesus to all generations, forever and ever, Amen"* (Ephesians 3:21).[39] In the balance of this chapter, I will briefly summarize the five major restoration movements up to the present day. For a through examination of the subject see Dr. Hamon's book *The Eternal Church.*

The Five Major Movements

All Christians who have received God's present truth accept these last five groups as restoration movements that were ordained of God. They are called major movements because **each one restored back into the Church truths and ministries that were lost during the Dark Ages of the Church.**

All Protestant Christians find their **roots** and present affiliation and function in one of these five groups.

Something practiced in the Church for the past six generations, does not, mean that it is biblically right. And then, something not practiced in your Church for the past six generations does not mean that it is biblically wrong.

Church historians have designated the year 1517 as the official beginning of the period of Church restoration. There have been five major movements since that time:

- The Protestant Movement (1500)—restored salvation by grace through faith (Ephesians 2:8-9).
- The Holiness Movement (1700)—restored sanctification, the church set apart from the world.
- The Pentecostal Movement (1900)—restored Holy Spirit baptism with unknown tongue.
- The Charismatic Movement (1960)—Renewal of all restored truth to all past movement churches. **Pastors** were restored to being sovereign head of their local churches.
- The Apostolic Movement[40](1990)—Apostolic leadership, release of miracles, networking, great harvest. **Apostle** ministry restored to bring order, finalize restoration of fivefold ministry for full equipping of the Saints.

New Truth to be revealed by the Holy Spirit (John 16:12-15)

There is a divine economy in the *process* of God's revelation of *truth* to believers. Jesus had *"many things"* (v.12), yet to say to His disciples, things the Holy Spirit would make known to them when the proper time came. Had He revealed them while He was with them, they would not have understood. But when the Holy Spirit came, HE would bring these unspoken truths to their minds.

> *"However, when He, the Spirit of truth, has come, He will **guide** you into all truth; for He will not speak on His own authority, but whatever He hears He will speak; and He will tell you things to come"*
>
> (v. 13).

The Holy Spirit would give them divine facts and the *truth* of those facts—and He would do it by a divinely arranged process. Notice that the Holy Spirit was to guide them into *"ALL TRUTH."* The disciples were given "all truth," and since God gave the Revelation to John on the Isle of Patmos, no other divine revelations have been given to men to be penned down as doctrine dictated by the Holy Spirit. Nothing remains to be added to the doctrine of the New Testament Church. The truth that the Holy Spirit would *make known* to the disciples would be sufficient for all generations.

"He will tell you things to come." The Holy Spirit would make known to the disciples all things relative not only to the Church Age—but even the ages beyond the Church Age. ALL truth, no exceptions!

- All we need to know about humankind, sin, salvation.
- All we need to know about God, God's Son, and the Holy Spirit.
- All we need to know about things that are to come.

We can find in the sixty-six books of our Bible. The Holy Spirit was not to speak of Himself but to bear witness of Jesus. His mission was to *glorify* God's Son, not Himself. *"He will take of what is Mine and declare it unto you"* (v. 14). The Holy Spirit shall take Christ's truth and reveal it to the disciples. Then by means of the Old and New Testament, the Spirit of Truth is even this day fulfilling these words to believers—and will continue to do so until the Church is taken out.

There are many glorious and wonderful things in the ages to come, things so glorious it is impossible for the finite mind to comprehend them. Paul says, "As it is written, eye has not seen, nor ear heard, nor have entered into the heart of man [or woman] the things which God has prepared for those who love Him. But God has revealed them to us through His Spirit. The Spirit searches all things, yes, the deep things of God" (1 Corinthians 2:9-10). Again, the Bible is given to all believers who seek to know and understand that divinely written truth, in each case, the Holy Spirit is the divine agent doing the work. (see 2 Peter 1:21). "All things that the Father has are Mine. Therefore I said that He will take Mine and declare it to you" (v. 1). This verse points out the perfect unity between Father, Son, and Holy Spirit.

The only possible way to understand the Scriptures is to be taught by the Holy Spirit. The Word of God is not learned in Bible Colleges under the teaching of earthly educators, although we should thank God for great men and women whom He has revealed many deep truths from the Scriptures. But these great people of God know such truths and are able to teach others only because the Holy Spirit has revealed them as they have dedicated themselves to the study of God's Word!

STUDY GUIDE: CHAPTER 15

STRENGTHENING THE RIGHT HAND OF GOD

1. The Book of Acts provides the _____ of the first century _____.

2. By His _____ and _____ Jesus fulfilled the law and the _____.

3. Church historians have designated _____ as the official beginning of the period of Church restoration.

4. The only way to understand the Scriptures is to be _____ by the _____.

5. All Protestant Christians find their _____ and present affiliations and functions in one of the Movement groups.

6. Who is the Spirit of Truth? _____

7. The word of God is not learned in Bible College under great teacher, but is _____ by _____ _____.

Chapter 16

EVERYONE MUST WITNESS

> Christian service means invading a battleground, not a playground; and you and I are the weapons God uses to attack and defeat the enemy. When God used Moses' rod, He needed Moses' hand to lift it. When God used David's sling, He needed David's hand to swing it. When God builds a ministry, He needs somebody's surrendered body to get the job done.
>
> Warren Wiersbe[41]

Some time ago a man, passing a church spotted his friend from work going in. The next day on the job, he said, "I didn't know you were a churchgoer." Oh yes, I have been for years now," he replied. "Really, it's funny you've always been ready to talk about anything, but you never said a word about God."

Why would anyone want to become a Christian if those who call themselves Christian aren't enthusiastic about it? I read some time ago of a comment made by Mahati Ghandi of India after observing Christians in America. In essence he was not impressed toward becoming a Christian because he felt that our walk was much different than our talk. Polls show that the majority of Christians never win a soul to Christ. In fact they never even try. Worse yet, as in the example above, many never let their neighbors, friends and fellow employees know that they are Christians. In Matthew 5:16, the Bible says,

"Let your light so shine
Before men, that they may
See your good works
And
Glorify your Father
in heaven."

One must ask the question, if a member doesn't witness; is he or she really a Christian? A Christian can't just sponge on Christianity. Jesus said,

"You are the salt of the earth;
But
If the salt loses its flavor,
How shall it be seasoned?
It is then
Good for nothing
But to be thrown out
And trampled
Underfoot by men"
(Matthew 5:13).

Salt is both a preservative and a flavor enhancer. No doubt its use as a preservative is what Jesus had mostly in view here. The Christian's godly life (witness) can preserve the Christian influence in the community for Christ.

The Witness of all believers

Somewhere along the way we have gone astray from the idea that every Christian is to witness. Many church members think of witnesses as those professionals on staff and those especially called to be missionaries.

It is worthy to note, when the early church was persecuted, the laity were all scattered abroad, but the leaders remained in Jerusalem (Acts 1:8). The Bible says, *"were scattered abroad went every* *where **preaching the Word**"* (Acts 8:4). In that same sense, every Christian is to be a witness, wherever he or she goes and in every thing is to be done in witness as unto the Lord. Again, the question is raised, "would a real Christian want to withhold from a lost world the "good news" that delivered him or her from death unto life?"

The *real test* of the value of Christianity, to the world looking on, is whether we are living its claims:

- Enjoying its fruit.
- Devoting our lives to spreading its message.

The unsaved want to know whether Christianity works in our homes, on our jobs, with our neighbors, and in our daily living. A true Christian does not become a witness—he or she is a witness, by what they are and how they live.

Witnessing on the Home Front

Many people are willing to witness and testify for Christ where people don't know them, but not to their neighbors and friends. Yet it is to them that they could witness best! Their friends could see the change in them and thereby know that the Gospel works:

- One could lie to strangers about his or her changed life, and they wouldn't know the difference.
- One could not lie to those whom he or she lives, works, and fellowships.

When Jesus gave the commission to the Church to preach the Gospel to every creature (Mark 16:15), He said that they were to start at home, then go to the community and then to the uttermost part of the earth. If a person can not witness at home and work, they will never be able to witness any where else. The story is told of one young man who wanted to be considered for foreign missionary service, but he could not get along with his neighbors. He was told that God could not use him anywhere in the world until he loved and witnessed to those people that knew him best. One writer suggests that there are only five ways to witness:

- By what he or she is.
- By what he or she does.
- By what he or she says.
- By what he or she gives.
- By what he or she prays.

We all should be ever mindful that the lost souls with whom you work or those that live next door to you are as lost as those any where in the world. God loves them as much as anyone. Jesus died for them. The same devil has them under bondage and they are heading to the same hell as any lost soul in the world.

Christian Grace

Christians are to live so that they establish the credibility of the Christian faith. The apostle Paul admonishes, *"Walk in wisdom toward those who are outside, redeeming the time. Let your speech always be* **with grace**, *seasoned with salt, that you may know how you ought to answer each one"* (Colossians 4:5-6). Speaking of those outside or unbelievers, in his writings Paul gives a list of graces that will enable the Christian to make the most of every evangelistic opportunity:

- Walk in wisdom before unbelievers (those outside).
- To speak what is spiritual, wholesome, fitting, kind, sensitive, purposeful, complimentary, truthful, loving, and thoughtful.
- Walk circumspectly, not as fools but as wise (Ephesians 5:15).
- Redeeming the time (Ephesians 5:16).
- But be filled with the Spirit (Ephesians 5:18).

The Christian's speech should act not only as a blessing to others, but as a purifying influence within the decaying society of the world.

STUDY GUIDE: CHAPTER 16

EVERY CHRISTIAN MUST WITNESS

1. All Christians should be enthusiastic about their _____.

2. Polls show that the _____ of _____ never win a soul to Christ.

3. Salt is both a _____ and a _____ _____.

4. When the early Church was persecuted they laity *"went everywhere* _____.

5. Jesus instructed, "begin _____ before witnessing anywhere else.

6. Christians are to live so that they establish the _____ of the Christian faith.

7. The Christian's speech should be a _____ _____ within the decaying society of the world.

NOTES

Chapter 1: God's Word, [His GPS]

1   The MacAuthur Study Bible (Study Notes on Romans 1)

Chapter 3: The Christian's secret Weapon

2   Edgar C. James, *Day of the Lamb,* (Victor Books 1984) 32.

3   Webster' New Explorer Dictionary (by Merriam-Webster Inc.) 1999

Chapter 4: The Abiding Word

4   Craig A. Carter, *Rethinking Christ and Cultur,* (by Brazos Press a Div of Baker Publishers) 107.
5   Derek Prince, *Foundational Truths,* (Charisma House, 2006) 12.
6   Francis J. Beckwith and Gregory Kould, *Relativism* (Baker Books) 20.
7   Ibid.
8   Ibid.

Chapter 5: The Spirit-filled Church

9   Charles A. Swindoll, *The Church Awakening* (Faith Words, 2010) 14.

10 Ibid. 14

11 Ibid. 15

12 The NKJV Study Bible (Study notes on Hebrews 4:12).

13 David Kinnaman, *You Lost Me* (Baker Books 2011) 99.

Chapter 6: Remember Who You Are

14 Nonie Darwish, *Cruel and Usual Punishment* (Thomas Nelson Inc. 2008) 245

15 Joshua Lingel, Jeff Morton, Bill Nikides, *Chrislam: How Missionaries Are Promoting An Islamized Gospel* (12 Minutes Publishing 2011) iii.

16 Adapted and modified from Alpha-Omega Ministries, Inc, *The Teacher's Outline & Study: Ephesians* (Leadership Ministries Worldwide 1996) 76.

17 Ibid. 79

18 Ibid. 81

19 Ibid. 83

20 Ray C. Stedman, *Body Life* (Thomas Nelson Publishers 1995) 27.

21 Ibid. 28

Chapter 9: Receiving the Promise of the Father

22 Kevin J. Conner, *The Foundationss of Christian Doctrine* (Bible Press, 1980) 79.

23 William Byron Forbush, *Fox's Book Of Martyrs* (Zondervan Publishing House, 22nd printing, 1967), 2.

24 Ibid. 5

25 Frank Bartleman, *Azusa Street,* (Bridge-Logos 1980) [April, 1925], xxvi

26 Ibid. xxvii

27 Ibid. xxix

Chapter 10: When Power comes to Church

28 Ray C. Steadman, *Body Life* (Thomas Nelson Publishers 1995), 73.
29 Charles E. Fuller Institute of Evangelism and Church Growth (Leader's Guide 1982), 2.

Chapter 13: Seeing Tomorrow Today

30 Jay R. Leach, *Give Me Jesus* (Trafford Publishing 2013) 232.
31 George B. Eager, *Winning Children to Christ* (The Mailbox Club, 1979) 9.
32 Kevin J. Conner, *The foundations of the Christian Doctrine* (Bible Press, 1980), 80.
33 Ibid. 80.

Chapter 14 Contend for the Faith

34 Dr. Bill Hamon, *The Day of the Saints* (Destiny Image Publishers, Inc. 2002), 150.
35 Ibid. 152.
36 Ibid. 153.
37 Ibid. 153.
38 Ibid. 153.
39 Ibid. 153.
40 Ibid. 154.

Chapter 15 Strengthening the Right Hand of God

41 Warren W. Wiersbe, *On Being a Servant of God,* (Baker Books, Grand Rapids, 2007), 46.